Education on Trial

NATHAN RUTSTEIN is currently Professor of Telecommunications at Springfield Technical Community College, a television journalist, TV documentary producer, lecturer and author. Formerly chairman of the University of Massachusetts School of Education Media/Telecommunications Department and a news editor with NBC and ABC News, he has acted as consultant to the White House Conference on children, advisor to Harlem Preparatory School and adjunct professor/consultant to Brazil's Institute for Space Research.

He is the author of *Go Watch TV*, *To Be One: A Battle Against Racism* and *Winning Spiritual Battles*, and other books. His most recent documentaries include *Finding a Solution* and *Black and White in Springfield*. He speaks regularly on the subject of combatting discrimination at universities across the USA, and has been instrumental in setting up more than 80 Institutes for the Healing of Racism in North America. This is his eighth book.

Books by the same author:

Go Watch TV!
   —What and How Much Should Children Watch?
He Loved and Served
Spirit in Action
To A Seeker
Corinne True
To Be One: A Battle Against Racism
Winning Spiritual Battles

EDUCATION ON TRIAL

Nathan Rutstein

ONEWORLD

OXFORD

Education on Trial
Oneworld Publications, Ltd.
(Sales & Editorial)
185 Banbury Road, Oxford
OX2 7AR, England

Oneworld Publications, Ltd.
(U.S. Sales Office)
County Route 9
P.O. Box 357
Chatham, NY 12037, USA

A CIP record for this book is available
from the British Library.

Printed and bound in Great Britain by
The Guernsey Press Co. Ltd.,
Guernsey, Channel Islands.

ISBN 1-85168-027-6

CONTENTS

ACKNOWLEDGMENTS

Considering my early encounters with formal schooling, I don't think anyone who knew me then would have predicted that I would one day write a book about education. But there have been certain people in my life who have made it possible. There is my mother, who never gave up on me, even though she had good reason to.

And there was Mrs. Fleming, my ninth grade English teacher, who saw a current of creativity in me that I was unaware of; her faith in me evolved into a source of inspiration that paved the way for me to become a writer.

Dwight Allen, who, as Dean of the School of Education at the University of Massachusetts, saw something in me that had the makings of a chairperson of one of his departments. It didn't matter to him that I was lacking the proper academic credentials for the job. Through that three-year experience I gained a close look at the inner workings of formal education in America.

Without the encouragement and liberal academic attitude of President Andrew Scebelli of Springfield Technical Community College, I wouldn't have been able to create a teaching approach and curriculum that has helped many students realize and develop potential they never knew they had.

If it wasn't for my wife Carol, I would never have attempted to write this book; for it was she who continually urged me to share with others what I have been able to achieve in the classroom. She felt strongly that others, especially teachers and parents, could benefit from what I had learned in my attempts to improve ways to educate the whole person.

Nathan Rutstein
Amherst, Massachusetts
November, 1991

INTRODUCTION

I have been teaching for 21 years, and will continue to teach until I'm told I must retire. I do it because I love doing it. There were opportunities to do other things, where the monetary rewards were far greater. One of the reasons I remain at Springfield Technical Community College is that I have the rare opportunity of being in a position to generate hope in men and women who don't have any; of acquainting them with their potential and helping them establish a means of developing it. For me, that's more exciting than discovering a diamond mine. Experiences like shedding tears of joy with parents who never expected a child of theirs to graduate from college, and witnessing an ex-convict finding his true self and life's purpose, and adopting me as his father — they are all priceless experiences that have enriched my soul.

Teaching has also been a great personal learning experience. I've learned about human behavior, a lot about myself, and how to reach and teach a variety of people. A driving desire to become a more effective teacher generated within me a growing curiosity about human nature. I have sought out psychologists, philosophers and educators whose views seem to make sense — and I have even read books on human behavior, recommended by my wife, Carol. I have also thought deeply and extensively about the appalling state of education in America and elsewhere, wondering what I could do to improve the continually worsening situation. I have ideas, some of which I've incorporated successfully in my classes; others deal with the general philosophy of education. For a long time I've hesitated sharing them with the public, because I have no stature in the world of pedagogy. Until this day I blush every time someone calls me a professor, for that title belongs, I have always felt, to a legitimate scholar, who holds a Ph.D. Considering my humble educational background, I still feel out of place among academicians,

especially when they confer in educationalese. Nevertheless, I
have been encouraged by some professionals and parents, from
North America and abroad, to share my views.

I offer them, not with the belief that they represent the
pedagogical panacea that humanity has been longing for — I
don't suffer from delusions of grandeur. They are offered in the
spirit of service, with the hope that sincere seekers of better ways
to teach might have more approaches and tools to choose from.
First, I feel, the whole notion of education has to be rethought
not only by educators, but also by parents, potential parents —
and everyone else. For, in the long run, a failing educational
system will hurt us all. The health of a community is dependent
on the health of its schools. Because more men and women of
all strata of society have become aware of this fact of life, a
loosely directed crusade, whipped up by disillusioned parents,
some disgruntled educators, and social activists, is being waged to
improve the quality of education. Fueling the flame of fervor of
this undertaking is the business world's clamor for a better
educated work force. Corporate chief operating officers know
that a poorly educated work force will adversely affect profits.
The New York Telephone Company reports that 115,000 of
117,000 applicants fail its employment exam. Some companies
have been forced to set up special remedial educational programs
— at great cost — to prepare prospective employees to work in
their factories and offices.

At this point, there's more decrying the seriousness of the
problem than constructive action. Oh, the media has
highlighted some encouraging experiments done in some
economically affluent communities, and in a few schools in
poor neighborhoods. But, for the most part, schools across
America have undergone little curriculum and teaching-
approach change. In many communities not enough money is
being allocated to purchase essential learning materials, let
alone finance research and development enterprises designed to
create teaching methods for students living in a world that's
very different from the one their teachers lived in when they
were children. Teacher morale remains low. There isn't the
incentive to change the existing academic pattern, because

_most teachers' time is devoted to dealing with students' dysfunctional behavior.

Discipline and attending to children's emotional problems — responsibilities teachers aren't trained to deal with — take up most of their energy and time, and they are losing the battle. Violence in our schools is growing, and spilling over to the community at large. As one frustrated American city official declared: "Some of our schools are becoming spawning grounds for criminality." In Britain Lord Griffiths, the Chairman of the Schools Examination and Assessment Council, claims the educational establishment must bear some of the responsibility for his nation's fractured moral backbone: "If you look at the kind of values they [students] come away with from some schools, it is frankly an absolute disgrace and responsible for the problems we have."

The moral breakdown in schools has become so bad that caveman disciplinary tactics are being praised by people in high positions. For example, in 1988, U.S. Secretary of Education William Bennett commended a New Jersey high school principal for wielding a baseball bat to maintain classroom order. The principal emerged as an overnight American hero. The same Secretary of Education has proposed that the solution to the slumping American education problem is a return to educational basics, with special emphasis on the contributions of western civilization. His rationale for this approach is that you should concentrate on what made you great.

The trouble with that reasoning is that the America of today is very different from the America of yesteryear. By the year 2000 more than 40% of the students attending public schools will be minorities, with heritage roots in Africa, Asia and Latin America. In that same year, less than 15% of all new jobs in the U.S.A. will be taken by white males. Methods and curriculum used in the "good old days," when 90% of the students were Christian and white, won't work. And America can no longer ignore the rest of the world. Its survival is dependent on other nations' resources, knowledge and goodwill. In order to thrive, it needs to respect and appreciate cultures other than those that evolved from western civilizations.

Even in Japan, which has emerged as the world's economic pace-setter, existing educational practices are being seriously questioned. A more open approach that stimulates creativity instead of stifling it is being called for. The present system is being blamed for the high suicide rate among students — and not producing enough original thinkers.

As the quality of education declines, many teachers of goodwill, who yearn to do the right thing in the classroom, are losing their enthusiasm for teaching. For them the educational future appears bleak. Obviously, ignoring the problem, or pretending it doesn't exist, won't help. And trying to improve what already exists won't work. A new approach is needed, one that's tailored to meet the demands of an emerging new world order.

An organic change is required in what is taught — and how it is taught. The teachers and curriculum must reflect an understanding of what a human being is, and a sensitivity to students' cultural backgrounds. The university departments that train teachers need the courage to abandon their outmoded methods and courses, many of which have been dressed up to appear up-to-date. They must prepare prospective teachers to understand what human potential is, and how to discover, release and develop it, as well as how to become artful communicators of knowledge.

They must share with prospective and practicing teachers the latest findings in brain research. Considerable evidence has been unearthed, for example, that the attitude and emotional state of the fetus' mother may be a factor in the development of a child's behavioral pattern; that the most fertile period of human intelligence development is between birth and age six; that there are at least seven forms of intelligence, ranging from mathematical and linguistic to musical; that intelligence is not only multifaceted, but it can also be increased; that there are left-brain and right-brain dominated learners among our students, requiring different teaching approaches.

And those who graduate from college education programs must know how to educate the whole human being, including the student's spiritual nature, from which springs moral strength.

Yes, the school teacher must bear some of the responsibility for a child's moral development. What I and like-minded men and women are calling for can be done. The resources are available — but most important, there's the crying need. To ignore the need is to commit social suicide.

Education isn't the only aspect of life today that's being reevaluated and forced to make fundamental changes. In politics and economics profound changes are taking place. In fact, bloodless revolutions have occurred in Eastern European countries which, as recently as two years ago, were tightly wedded to Marxism. Now these nations are searching for a more effective, democratic means of governance. In Western Europe, twelve nations, some of them bitter enemies in two world wars, are forming an economic and political union. Nations in Southeast Asia are planning to do the same thing. Women — worldwide — are making headway in their quest for equality with men. More people around the world are emerging out of the cocoon of nationalism with a global awareness, calling for internationally orchestrated solutions to universal problems such as environmental pollution and disarmament — and meaningful progress is being made on both fronts. There's a growing world consciousness — and altruism. When famine strikes the Sudan and Ethiopia, or a killer-earthquake rocks Soviet Armenia, governments and people in different parts of the world respond with assistance, without being asked.

Fundamental changes are being made in the business world. Rank and file employees are participating more in the direction of the companies they work for. More and more firms have adopted industrial profit-sharing schemes. Many companies are extending their operations into different countries, causing an unprecedented social mix of different ethnic groups. There's a more open and freer exchange of goods and ideas between peoples.

Even in the lofty world of physics dramatic changes are occurring. Physicists are discovering aspects of reality that their predecessors weren't aware of. The new age physicists have scrapped the mechanistic view of our world, the universe and the order of life for a more fluid one, declaring that all of creation is interconnected, interrelated, that the universe and the human being don't function like machines, a belief that shaped the reductionist scientific philosophy, which dominated western thinking for more than three centuries and influenced the development of our present day failing educational systems.

We now know that it is the whole that determines the behavior of the parts, and not the other way around. Today's educational approaches and curricula, for the most part, are based on the assumption that the parts determine the behavior of the whole. As a result, most schools divide knowledge into segments. To continue to pursue this pedagogical structure is to go against the grain of the principle that all things in life are interrelated.

Even though many now recognize that a new world order is upon us — granted, it is in its formative stage — educational systems around the world pursue their responsibilities the way they did a century ago. The changes made have been largely superficial. Reforming what is fundamentally flawed won't work — an organic change is required. While this book attempts to show why the prevailing educational systems are failing, it also tries to describe the organic change it calls for. In doing this, I have primarily the practicing and prospective teachers in mind, as well as parents. My aim is to help them turn their classrooms and homes into vital learning centers, dedicated to preparing students to live and work effectively in our new world order. To achieve this end, I draw upon my experiences in the educational arena, both as a student and as a teacher. In order to reveal how a prevailing educational system can easily miss opportunities to help a child become an effective learner, I carefully reviewed my experience in school. Upon reflection, I decided to share publicly what I had discovered, with the hope of helping teachers avoid the mistakes made with me.

I also describe my work teaching at an urban community college, which has been my most professionally gratifying experience. I have been fortunate in being able to explore important issues such as the role of the teacher in the way students learn, and the way confidence and feelings of self-worth affect the learning process. Since ability plus attitude equals achievement, a way of overcoming student feelings of inferiority has been developed and is being successfully employed. Students learn who they really are and how to discover, release and develop their potential to the fullest. Over the years I have developed a human development curriculum — through intuition, reflection and experimentation — which has been integrated into our curriculum. It stresses, among other things, social values in the classroom — such as creating a spirit of familyhood and emphasizing cooperation over competition, teamwork over individual striving for success — that will stand students in good stead in their future work environment where such values on the part of the individual are highly beneficial to the whole. The stress on qualities and talents beyond the purely academic helps students to feel valued as the multi-talented and able individuals they all can be. The process is described in such a way that adventurous educators, teaching at all levels, could apply it to their own programs, whether here in America or overseas.

What I have done requires no extra outlay of funds. Any teacher, with an open mind and a sincere desire to help his or her students grow intellectually and socially, is capable of achieving the results we have witnessed. My hope is that by being exposed to the contents of this book, teachers' enthusiasm for their calling will be sparked, that they will gain some of the guidance and confidence they have sought in recent years — to do the kind of job they really want to do.

PART ONE

REEVALUATING EDUCATION

CHAPTER ONE

A Low Achiever

Although I never did well in school, I had a certain reverence for formal education. Maybe being a child of Russian-Jewish immigrants had something to do with that. My parents viewed America as the promised land. To them it was truly the "land of the free and the home of the brave."

After passing through the Ellis Island Immigration Center, they never wavered about their decision to leave the "old country." Living in Russia was hard: it wasn't only the rabid anti-semitism, the pogroms, the hunger and the lack of fuel during the harsh winters — there were also no opportunities to improve their lives, and no time to contemplate the future. In Russia, in the early 1920s, surviving was the only purpose to life for my parents, and the millions of others like them.

"In America," my father would often say, "you can become somebody." He and my mother believed that school was the springboard to success. They marveled over the fact that their children could receive a free education; and they were determined to take advantage of such a wonderful opportunity.

Now, their appreciation for education had little to do with the love of knowledge. To them schooling was an avenue to a secure job, a ticket to respectability, something they always wanted but couldn't achieve in the land of their birth. They dreamed of their son becoming a doctor or a lawyer. Though my parents made sure I attended school every day, and looked presentable, they had no appreciation for scholarship, a practice that was foreign to them. Maybe that's why we only had two books in our house while I was attending elementary school. One of the books was won by my mother in a lottery the local movie house held weekly. It was the letter G volume of a set of encyclopedia. The other book was purchased by my father, who never read it. I remember when he bought it. I was around nine at the time.

Actually, I was surprised that my father did what he did. For he had a rule of never buying anything from door-to-door salesmen; except the salesman who sold my father the book looked nothing like the peddlers he was accustomed to — disheveled looking men, usually immigrants pushing pants, lingerie, socks and men's underwear. The book salesman, however, was tall, blond, blue-eyed, wearing a finely pressed light blue suit with a perfectly ironed shirt and a golden tie. He was also polite, and when he spoke he sounded like someone whose ancestors came over on the Mayflower. When my father handed the man money, he really wasn't buying a book, he was trying to buy acceptance into what he felt was "real America."

Though I never read the book, I remember its title — *Watchtower*. And I also remember some of the pictures inside, of smiling men and women, looking very much like the salesman, with wings instead of arms. About a year later I learned that the proper term for those figures was angels.

Though as a youngster I struggled with my school work, I admired my teachers. In fact, I viewed them as superhuman creatures. This became clear to me in the fifth grade. After lunch one day, I ran back to the school yard where all students had to assemble in front of their teachers in two straight lines. Standing in the usual spot was my teacher, except this time she was doing something I didn't expect of teachers — she was munching on a chocolate bar. A teacher eating candy! I thought. That can't be. Ordinary people do things like that!

Only now do I understand why I was such a poor student. A dreamer by nature, I found reading, writing and arithmetic as they were taught in New York City's public school number 77 boring, a waste of time. While the teachers addressed our class, I dreamt of searching for treasure in far away places (I liked geography), hitting home runs like Joe DiMaggio of the New York Yankees, or fighting injustice like the Green Hornet, the leading character of a popular radio program in the 1930s. My day dreaming was also an exercise in wonderment: I wanted to know what caused rain and snow; I wanted to know what made the sun shine; I wanted to know what made birds fly and fish swim; I wanted to find a way to reach the moon. I wanted to know if there really was a God. My curiosity wasn't satisfied in the classroom. Mainly because the things I wondered about were rarely mentioned by my teachers, and besides, I was too scared to approach them. For I sensed they didn't like me; that they had already made up their minds that I was one of those dull students who wouldn't "amount to much." When I used to think about my teachers, all my inner eye would see were red correction marks on my exam papers. In a way, they planted in my mind the idea that I was dumb.

Now, I know they didn't mean to do that; nor were they aware of the pain that caused me as a child and youth. You see, as a child I always respected my teachers' opinions, because they went to college, they were professionals, they had the power to pass or fail me and they didn't make mistakes. So when I, as an eighth grader, thought about my future, the idea of being dumb influenced what I tried to envision. I had doubts as to whether I could be what most of my classmates wanted to be. Therefore in school I never thought seriously about what I wanted to be. For me the image of my future was fuzzy, actually, a mishmash of raw wishes, fears and doubts. Yet when adults asked me what I wanted to be, I would respond with something that I knew would impress them: "a doctor," I would say. In my neighborhood a physician commanded greater respect than the President of the United States. To a few relatives and close family friends who were aware of my budding artistic ability I revealed that I was planning on becoming an art director for films, something I knew nothing about. The idea came to me one day while watching the credits of a movie. It all seemed so logical: I like movies; I could draw fairly well; and all the adults I knew had the highest regard for film-makers. But what they didn't know was my real ambition — becoming a major league baseball player. That I felt was a realistic way of achieving fame and fortune.

Fortunately, there was something within me that resisted the notion that I was stupid. Without that deeply felt belief I think I would have bowed to the wisdom of the school educators. I almost succumbed in the ninth grade. At that time I was living in Mt. Vernon, a northern suburb of New York City. The junior high school guidance counselor asked to meet with my father and I. She wanted to chart my academic course for the next three years.

She was a pleasant woman, gray haired and polite, with all of the proper educational credentials and an outstanding reputation in her field. I could tell how my father, who was dressed in his best suit, felt in the presence of this "real American." He was in awe of her and would try his best to implement whatever advice she would give in regards to my academic future.

In a gentle way, she revealed to him and me that I didn't have the capacity to do college work. She had solid evidence to prove her point. When she handed my father the results of my aptitude and intelligence tests, he tried to pretend that he understood what was before him.

"So what do you think Nathan should do?" said my father, handing the papers back to the guidance counselor.

"Air-conditioning is an up and coming field. He could take a vocational course and when he graduates he'll be able to secure a good job," she said.

I refused to take her advice. I signed up for the college bound high school course without telling my father, who would have been furious had he known what I had done. In retrospect, I now know why I defied the counselor's decision and lied to my father. First, there was that belief I had buried in my heart, that somehow I would eventually succeed. As a child and youth I had no idea how that feeling came about, nor did I wonder about its origin. All I knew then was that it was most prominent outside of school.

But as an adult I needed to know where that feeling stemmed from, and I found out. My mother cultivated that belief in me. I doubt if it was something that she had planned to do. I say that because she's not a person who sets goals; she's a skillful survivor who reads on a fourth grade level. I don't think she ever read more than 10 pages of the book she won at the movie house lottery.

It was her love instinct that motivated her to encourage me to succeed. She had no idea of what I should be "when I grew up." All she knew was that I was a good person and she kept telling me that, along with giving me hugs and kisses. She focused on the good things I did, not the bad. And she would often rescue me from my father, who like most of my teachers, had a tendency to criticize whatever I did, or belittle me by calling me "worthless," "fool" or "Layminum Goylum" — a Yiddish term for someone who can't do anything right. I suspect he had a good reason to feel that way, because of my performance whenever he ordered me to assist him with his work. He was a plumber, something I knew I didn't want to be. Though it was good money, I couldn't see myself twisting snake wire down toilets for the rest of my life. He couldn't understand why I wasn't enthusiastic on the job; and he would explode every time I would flub — and that was often.

On the other hand whenever my mother told me that I would succeed, or that I was good, she would say it with deep conviction. So when I succeeded in sports, she would always say, "See, I told you so." Every time the newspaper reported on my athletic exploits, she would cut the article out and proudly show it to her friends. It didn't matter that she couldn't distinguish between a baseball and a football and never saw me play a game.

There was another reason why I refused to take the vocational course. It was what Mrs. Fleming, my ninth grade English teacher shared with me and the rest of the class. Incidentally, she and Mrs. Pardie, my fifth grade teacher, are the only teachers whose names I remember. (Mrs. Pardie was the teacher I spotted eating a chocolate bar.) Mrs. Fleming had a practice of predicting what each of her ninth grade students would end up doing professionally. Had I known what day she

would carry out her exercise in prophecy, I would have feigned
sickness and stayed home.

It was a sunny, warm day in early June when Mrs. Fleming
made her prognostications. Because our English class met during
the last period of the school day my mind was usually focused
elsewhere (on that day the baseball field, a few miles down the
road) but it snapped back to the classroom when she announced
that "this is the day we look into your future."

I cringed. "Oh, no," I said to myself, "if only I could escape."
Luckily, she started with the boys and girls on the other side of
the room. I would be among the last to be sentenced. I swear I
don't remember any of the predictions she made of the other
students. And I know why: I was so fearful of what she was going
to say about me I couldn't hear anything but my heartbeat.

Finally, my time came. I bowed my head when she
mentioned my name, and closed my eyes and squeezed the
baseball glove on my lap. I knew every eye in the place was on
me, even the girl I liked very much but never shared my feelings
with.

"Nathan," Mrs. Fleming said, pausing purposely (I thought to
prolong the torture), "You could become a writer."

I looked up at the trim, attractive blond woman, and I knew
she meant it. There was no smirk on her "real American" face,
and she wasn't teasing me. Though she waited for me to
respond, I had nothing to say. I was caught off guard — too
surprised to say anything. She had planted a brilliant idea in my
mind, one that I never forgot. But though I was deeply
impressed with what she said, it didn't cancel out or supplant the
negative ideas of myself that I had learned in all of the other
classes I attended through the years. Still, I left school that day
full of joy, full of hope, hopped on my bicycle and headed for the
baseball field, replaying in my mind what Mrs. Fleming had said
not only to me but the entire class. It felt better than hitting a
home run. But by the time I reached the field, doubts started to
plague me: "Me — a writer?" I said to myself. "How could that
be when I couldn't tell the difference between a colon and a
semicolon?" I was barely passing English. Mrs. Fleming had
given me a D on my last report card. Besides she could be

wrong, I thought. It was her word against the word of all the other teachers I had had during my nine years in school.

No other teacher in high school saw in me what Mrs. Fleming saw. Consequently, with the exception of my first semester in the tenth grade, school became a battleground again. It was me pitted against the school system that had branded me a "low achiever."

Why did I get two B+s and two Bs in the first semester of the tenth grade, in courses like Latin, Algebra, Biology and American History? I needed to prove to my ninth grade guidance counselor that she was wrong about me. But more important I needed to prove to myself that she was wrong about me. So I did my homework — and actually studied. And I did it, even though I didn't have my own desk at home and hated to read. Because my reading comprehension level was low, I had to labor over passages, rereading them time and time again. I don't think it was a case of being dyslexic and not knowing it. It was a case of not growing up in a home where books were cherished and parents read regularly, and enjoyed doing it. I wasn't trained to appreciate literature; I didn't know how it could enrich my life. Because I had so much trouble reading, I developed a prejudice toward it. I often refused to read instructions to tests, applications and every form I encountered, which caused all sorts of difficulties for me. To this day I am a slow reader.

As a child I yearned for recognition and respect. Since I wasn't getting it in the classroom, and not getting enough at home, I found what I thought I needed in the sand lots and streets of the Bronx neighborhood where I lived the first thirteen years of my life. In my neighborhood I could run faster than any other kid. I loved beating the teacher's pets and the smart kids. And none of my classmates could match my fence climbing prowess, nor my boxing ability. It wasn't that I enjoyed knocking people out; it was doing something better than someone else that gave me a great deal of satisfaction.

I worked at becoming a good boxer. On Friday nights I would listen to the main event from Madison Square Garden, turning my room into a ring and throwing every punch the announcer declared my favorite fighter threw. Going fifteen rounds was quite a workout. But I didn't mind, because after a few months I noticed progress — and that made me happy. My punches were being delivered with greater speed, accuracy and power. Some of the school bullies could attest to that. In the seventh grade I had earned the unofficial title of the best fighter in the neighborhood. Even high schoolers recognized that. And so did a professional boxing trainer who tried to persuade me to seriously consider turning "pro" when I reached eighteen. He wanted me to join his stable of "future champs."

My reputation followed me to Mt. Vernon. I made sure of that, by provoking a few open handed matches in the street with a few of the neighborhood boys. After reddening their faces with solid shots, they spread the word about my fisticuff skills throughout the junior high school I transferred to.

But I had to pay a price for my fame. When someone from a different neighborhood would appear on our street to terrorize one of my friends, I was expected to confront the guy. There were times when I would be called away from the dinner table to defend my honor and reputation. And there were times when I felt terribly overmatched — like the time the biggest kid in school came looking for me, accompanied by four of his followers. Evidently he wanted to prove to them that he was king of the school. A friend, who later became a successful lawyer, found me in my backyard. When he told me who the challenger was I wanted to pretend that I had something else to do. But I didn't dare do that, because that would have been construed as "chickening out." So I followed him to the street corner where the Goliath was waiting for me, looking huge and formidable. He was sixteen, and I was fourteen. He was at least five inches taller than me and his biceps were fully developed and big. His yellow T-shirt seemed like it was painted on his V-shaped body. I wasn't only scared about being knocked out; my image would be destroyed if the guy beat me up.

My friend, who volunteered to be my second, ran home to get his brother's boxing gloves. Henry, my opponent, sneered at me; so did his followers. We didn't exchange a word.

No rules were established for the bout; and there was no referee. We were going to fight on the street corner where we were standing until one of us gave up. After our gloves were laced, Henry started throwing wicked left and right roundhouse punches that didn't land. That was encouraging, I thought. He didn't know how to defend himself. His midsection was wide open for my left hooks. After the second shot, he bent over, clutching his abdomen, a prime target for an uppercut. But I didn't throw it, for I sensed that Henry knew he was through.

The following day in school boys and girls were talking about what I had done to Henry. I enjoyed that; and I enjoyed guys coming up to me to shake my hand. That made up for being humiliated in the classroom; no one would dare make fun of me if I misspelled a word or couldn't solve a math problem. Boxing had been good to me.

But there were other sports I liked better — especially baseball. The first summer in Mt. Vernon I found myself playing for the Blue Sox, a team composed of some of the better 14-year-old players in the city. Our manager, Bill Real, who had played professionally for the Yankee organization, was probably the finest baseball coach in the area. He had a knack for finding and developing talent. My friends and neighbors were impressed that I had been selected to play for the Blue Sox.

A year later I was invited to a Brooklyn Dodger try out camp in Yonkers. George Sisler, the Hall of Famer and chief Dodger scout at the time, and his assistants approached me after I hit a few balls over the fence. When they discovered I was only fifteen, they shied away from talking to me about signing a contract. You had to be at least eighteen to sign. But they kept in touch. First, arranging for me to become part of the Westchester Dodger All Stars, a team made up of the best college and high school players in the county. And I was invited to workout in Ebbets Field, the stadium where the Dodgers played their home games.

My reason for going to college had nothing to do with acquiring knowledge or learning a profession. I wanted to go because my friends were going. Staying home, I feared, would make me a social outcast.

Despite my poor grades, I was admitted to college. Being able to hit a baseball far helped me get into the University of

Alabama. When I arrived on campus, I was greeted by two leaders of a fraternity, who treated me like a celebrity. In 1949, athletes on many campuses were considered heroes. They escorted me —carrying my bags all the way — to the fraternity house where I was to live while attending the university. Waiting for me was Don Keats, another northern athlete, who was to be my roommate, and would eventually become my closest friend in Alabama.

Both of us had a benefactor at the university. Bubba Brown owned the leading department store in Tuscaloosa; and we were to go to him if we needed clothing or spending money or guidance in solving our social and economic problems. I met Bubba Brown once; he was a gentle, gracious, soft-spoken man with a rich southern accent. I never asked him for a thing. Neither did Don.

We didn't stay in the fraternity long. Our departure had nothing to do with the individual members — they were all friendly and helpful. And the cooking was first class, thanks to Tammy, the cook, a black woman whose last name I never got to know. All my attempts to get to know her were rebuffed by her. There seemed to be an impenetrable invisible wall between us. At the time I didn't know that breaking through the wall would have led to her being fired. There were other objections to living in the fraternity house. Being a democrat at heart, I despised elitism; and the senseless initiation rituals that all first year students had to undergo were ridiculous.

Moving to the dormitory was like moving into a city housing project. It was noisy, messy and a haven for grafittists. Still, I felt a lot more comfortable there than at the fraternity house. The only thing I missed was Tammy's cooking.

Strangely, the bright spot of my University of Alabama stay was my classroom experience. I passed all four subjects (Biology, English Composition, Western Civilization and R.O.T.C — "Reserve Officers Training Corps" — which was mandatory for all able-bodied males). Two C+s and two Cs. At the time I wasn't impressed with the fact that I could do college work. I was more concerned with making the basketball team. After two workouts, Don and I decided to transfer to a school that played a

fastbreak style of basketball. Though we set up tryouts at a
number of universities in the North, we ended up transferring to
a college we didn't visit — DePauw University, in Greencastle,
Indiana. I think it was the friendly tone of the Admissions
Director's letters that convinced us to go there. I'm sure passing
all of my courses at the University of Alabama helped me to be
admitted to DePauw, a place where I would discover new
personal possibilities and overcome some deep-rooted negative
impressions of myself.

When I unpacked my bags in my dormitory room, I wasn't
thinking about exploring the library or the physics labs, I was
thinking about stepping into the batter's box of the baseball field
which was on the other side of the campus. But my attitude
gradually changed.

How I became a real student is difficult to pinpoint. But the
fact that that happened can't be denied. I think being in a
different environment was a factor: the students and faculty in
Indiana weren't aware of my "low achiever" reputation in New
York. While I was still haunted by it, Mrs. Fleming's insight and
my mother's blind faith in me encouraged me to make an effort
to try to succeed in the classroom. True, my educational
foundation was weak, but my new attitude helped. I was no
longer afraid to take the teacher aside after class, or go to his
office, and have him explain something I didn't understand. It
was at DePauw that I learned the difference between a colon and
a semicolon.

I discovered poetry. Oh, I had wrestled with it in high
school, finally brushing it aside as something sissies liked. But in
college I learned to love it. And that happened because I had to
write it. The more I wrote the more I wanted to read. I
pondered poets like Blake, Yeats, Tennyson and Byron; and T.S.
Eliot became my hero. I actually derived pleasure from reading
good poetry. It wasn't only the aesthetic charge that moved me;
I was also intrigued by style. Through poetry I was introduced to
analytical thinking. And something else: while writing a poem
one day I realized what Mrs. Fleming had seen in the written
ramblings I did in her class — it was raw creative power. She
spotted potential I wasn't aware of.

Some of my poems were good enough to be printed in the university literary journal, a 20-page mimeographed tract containing some students' poems, short stories and essays. For me, gaining that kind of notoriety felt better than driving in the winning run in the bottom of the ninth inning. I was entering a different world, and I liked what I saw and felt. I had friends that didn't know the difference between a batting average and a pitcher's earned run average. A few months later one of my short stories was selected to appear in the journal.

Now my room-mate Don, an athlete's athlete, who did 100 push-ups every night before going to bed, showed no concern over my new-found literary interests. But when he learned that I was going to play a major role in The Medium, a Gian Carl Menotti opera (I played Toby, a deaf mute) he asked to have a man-to-man talk with me. I know he had my best interest at heart when he warned me about the possibilities of losing my manhood.

Favorable revues in the college newspaper helped me land leading roles in other plays like George Bernard Shaw's St. Joan. I had discovered my latent hunger for creative expression. And it was an insatiable hunger, because nothing I created was completely satisfying. I kept writing. In fact, I did more writing than hitting baseballs. And I kept reading, but only material I knew I would like — poetry, short stories and history. I gravitated to the late night dormitory philosophical discussions, holding my own with even the Phi Beta Kappa prospects. I was immersed in the ocean of intellect, and finding it refreshing.. At one of those discussions I was told about the annual campus oratorical contest, and urged to compete. I had never given a speech, nor was I ever inclined to give one. Yet the idea of doing it intrigued me. But what to talk about? I knew it had to be something topical. At the time, Senator Joseph McCarthy was waging a crusade against "leftist" professors who he felt were poisoning the minds of America's impressionable youth. Because I was appalled by his witchhunt tactics, and disagreed with his premise, I decided to speak on academic freedom. Writing it was a snap. I guess when you feel strongly about something you're not prone to suffer from "writer's block." Since the speech had to be memorized, my drama experience came in handy.

When I walked into the room where all of the other contestants were waiting to be called, an urge to flee swept over me. Sitting there, serious, almost sullen, they seemed formidable, especially the guys wearing ties. I knew some of them. They weren't phonies — like me. They were legitimate scholars, destined to be professors, scientists and lawyers. I felt like a fly-weight in the ring with a heavyweight. When my time came to enter the adjoining room where the judges sat, I wasn't sure I wanted to walk in that direction.

The judges were all professors and all male; only one of them was younger than 50. From the lectern they seemed ominous. What was more frightening was not remembering a thing I had prepared. I almost panicked. But it all came back immediately after a speech professor introduced me to the panel. Though I hadn't flubbed, I left the room certain I hadn't won, or even come close to winning; and certain I would never try something like that again, for I felt I had made a fool of myself. Not a judge had uttered a word after I completed my talk.

The next day I received a call to meet with the judges. When I was told that I had won the competition, I really felt that someone was playing a terrible joke. Though the professor on the other end of the phone was amused at my reaction, he insisted that I had won and asked if I would represent DePauw in the state collegiate oratorical contest. Of course, I said I would.

No victory in my life was as meaningful to me as winning the campus oratorical contest; for I had done well in an aspect of life I seriously doubted I could do well in. It was like being freed from a cage. In my euphoric state, which lasted about a week, I found myself more articulate, more productive academically, more creative. During that period I produced the best paper of my college career. It was for an English class on idiom development, in which I analyzed baseball terminology. My professor found the paper "penetrating and funny," liking especially the section about our team's coach whom he knew and admired as a renaissance man. In that section I described him completely absorbed in the game, with his hands cupped around his mouth, exhorting our pitcher to do well, except the language he used had meaning only to a player or a fanatical fan: "zip that pill by 'em, baby!" which loosely translated means, "strike out the batter."

I never forgot the joyous feeling winning the oratorical contest set off in me. Joy, I learned, makes our intellect keener. (Later in life, when I found myself in a teaching situation, I tried hard to make learning a joy for students, especially for those who didn't think they could do well in school.)

Though I didn't win the state contest, the oratory experience helped me win greater self-esteem, as well as respect from my father. When he received the newspaper clipping concerning my campus triumph, my mother said he read it and wept. He even sent me a congratulatory note, something he never did when I excelled in the sports arena.

I learned something else at DePauw. Not from a classroom lecture or a chat with a professor. It was from a friendship with two students, who, I'm sure, hadn't planned to give me what turned out to be the greatest gift of my life — an awareness of my spiritual nature.

Bill Allison and Bill Smits were close friends. Allison was a lanky black Georgian with a keen interest in scholarship; Smits was a slight white Chicagoan with the vision and heart of a poet. I got to know them under depressing circumstances.

On the first Tuesday of November, 1952, I was sitting alone in one of the union building's lounges, brooding over the result of the presidential election. I had just turned off the radio. Listening to Adlai Stevenson's concession speech was painful; I really felt that humanity would suffer some serious setbacks and never recover because of my hero's loss that night. When Allison and Smits entered the lounge, they noticed me. Originally, I wanted to be alone, but seeing them I had a change of heart, and I waved them over. They drew up chairs and we chatted; except I did most of the talking and they listened, listening mostly with the heart. I needed the opportunity to release my frustration and vent my anger, and they were willing to be my sounding board. Though they didn't share my pessimism, they didn't try to prove how wrong my assessment of life was. While walking back to the dormitory together, I realized that my mood had changed.

On the surface I had little in common with Allison and Smits. They were serious students with little interest in sports, whereas I had just wandered into the world of intellect, awed, knowledge-starved and uncertain about my presence there. I sought them out, because of the feeling I had while in their midst. Their optimism was infectious. With them around I felt more hopeful. Their language was clean, never laced with sarcasm. If they had something to say about someone, it was usually positive. For me that was a switch. I had been brought up believing that life was mean, a jungle; and if backbiting was necessary to get what you wanted you engaged in it without qualms. Overcoming that practice wasn't easy for me. In their presence I felt good about myself.

As I look back at those days, I can now appreciate what that good feeling was. I was discovering my spiritual nature. Yet if anyone had tried to tell me that, at the time, I would have laughed in his face and avoided his company. Allison and Smits were wise; they never tried.

The fact that Allison was black and Smits white didn't escape me. Seeing them together was an unusual sight on campus because of an unofficial social code that everyone adhered to, namely, Blacks had to know their place; they couldn't join a fraternity; dating a white woman was taboo, and real black and white friendships weren't encouraged. But Allison and Smits had a real friendship. I don't think they felt that courage was required to maintain their relationship. But I did. It was 1952.

Because I was impressed with them, I wanted to know what made them so special, what made me want to be with them. Allison and Smits were members of the Bahá'í Faith. A year after graduation I became a Bahá'í in Okinawa. By that time I knew that to be truly educated our spiritual nature as well as our brain and body required development. In time, I learned how to do that.

CHAPTER Two

Different Kinds of Intelligence

I learned a lot after college, especially about people like myself who did poorly in school. We learn best by doing, and absorb knowledge more readily if it's related to real life issues and problems. We're also more proficient in employing "street smarts" (a form of common sense) than the average "book worm." That became evident during my U.S. Army basic training at Fort Dix, in New Jersey.

Most of us were draftees from metropolitan New York City, possessing a highly cultivated scheming mentality. None of us liked being soldiers. It seems that the most brilliant schemes to get out of the Army were developed by the least educated.

Joe, who had worked as a messenger for a successful bookie in lower Manhattan, wanted to be back home to help support his widowed mother whose cataracts kept her from working. A deep distrust of any form of officialdom kept him from filing a request for a hardship discharge with the company commander, whom Joe viewed as his enemy. Instead, he created his own way of winning his freedom. He launched a campaign to convince his superiors that he was unfit to serve in the Armed Forces in any capacity. Joe assumed the role of company "fool" from the very first day our platoon's sergeant (a career soldier) set eyes on him.

Joe was only five-foot-three and of slight build. He wore everything a soldier was supposed to wear, but he wore them in a strange fashion. The peak of his fatigue hat, for example, was always over his right ear. Somehow he found a trench coat that would fit a six-footer comfortably, and wore it whenever we were ordered out of barracks. In that coat no one could see his hands or scuffed boots. And he never used the belt. So when he marched with the rest of us, he dragged the belt and the bottom of the coat along the ground. Since he only shaved every third day, he seemed to need a shave most of the time. After seeing him march several times, his fellow draftees dubbed Joe "the Old Testament."

Because he never sassed the sergeant or ridiculed him, Joe was never placed in the stockade. Part of his campaign called for giving the impression that he was sincerely trying to carry out all orders, but was incapable of executing them properly. The sergeant, who was from Kentucky, and took everything at face value, had no idea of Joe's plot. He fell into the trap Joe had set. "The Old Testament" became the company "odd ball." Whenever the sergeant wanted to explain how not to do something he would point to Joe, thus reinforcing Joe's contention that he wasn't mentally or physically fit to be a soldier.

But it took much more persistence and creativity for Joe to achieve his goal. For a whole week he would sit up in bed at around three in the morning and scream "the bugs are coming, the bugs are coming!" Then he would slide his foot locker to the edge of the stairwell and push it down stairs. When the locker hit the floor below, the sergeant would dash out of his room, in his underwear, like a trooper trying to find a foxhole during an enemy artillery barrage. None of the draftees complained, because we knew what Joe was up to and we wanted him to succeed.

It took six weeks for Joe's carefully thought out scheme to produce the result he envisioned. His performance on the firing line convinced our company commander that Joe was a menace not only to himself but to everyone around him. I don't think I'll ever forget that momentous occasion in Joe's life. He was in

a prone position, draped in his trenchcoat, and waving his rifle at
the target. Everyone but the sergeant scrambled for cover.
When Joe squeezed the trigger of the weapon he had never
cleaned, an orange flash and smoke shot out of the barrel. As for
the bullet, no one knew where it landed. One thing was certain,
it didn't hit any part of the target. Joe dropped the smoking rifle
and stood up, literally shaking in his boots. In seconds, the
company commander drove up and demanded an explanation.
The sergeant had one — a long list of Joe's blunders, which
turned out to be the rationale for the "Old Testament's"
discharge from the Army.

I never saw Joe again. I suspect he thrived in the world he
knew best, probably becoming a successful bookie; and at
appropriate times gleefully shared with those he trusted how he
outsmarted Uncle Sam.

In revealing Joe's colorful Army experience, I am not trying
to glorify his escapades in the military, or condone deception as
credible behavior. It is, rather, to illustrate that those who don't
succeed in school are not bereft of intelligence, creativity,
discipline and self-control. What Joe organized and carried out
in six weeks at Fort Dix is the kind of stuff that chief operating
officers hail in corporate board rooms as "creative and persistent
efficiency," the kind of efficiency that leads to promotions and
leadership positions. It is a pity that Joe's brilliance was never
noticed by his teachers. Chances are that if it had been, he
would have been encouraged to further his education and would
have contributed meaningfully to his community. Sadly, through
the years, there have been, and still are, many men and women
like Joe, not only in America but worldwide.

Consider what Joe had to do to achieve his goal. He created
a phased plan that took into account every conceivable obstacle.
It also took an uncanny insight into human behavior, and
restraint, to avoid being thrown into the stockade. And without
his dogged determination, he would have failed to successfully
carry out his plan. Only once did he let up on his role — and
that was the day he went home. It was an overcast day, a raw
drizzle fell. Joe, dressed in civilian clothes and carrying an
umbrella, walked to the barracks door, stopped and turned to us

— most of us were sitting on our beds or lockers — and winked. When he stepped outside, he opened his umbrella and never looked back.

I had a personal experience in the Army that reinforced the idea that there are many kinds of intelligences. Scoring high on a Scholastic Aptitude Test is not the only one. That became evident when we had to tear down and reassemble our rifles. Even some Ivy Leaguers solicited help from guys who had operated jack hammers and bulldozers for a living. The one who helped me came from Manhattan's Hell's Kitchen, a tough Irish neighborhood on the borough's west side. Francis, who never finished high school, had been a truck driver for a local Coca Cola bottling company. Besides being a mechanical whiz, he was an exceedingly patient person. He had to be to teach me how to assemble weapons. If it wasn't for Francis I would have continually failed platoon inspection and been relegated to washing pots and pans on weekends while everyone was on pass.

But I was able to help Francis in a different way. When he entered the Army, his teeth were in bad shape. In fact, they were so bad, a Fort Dix dentist yanked every tooth from his head. For two weeks he ate nothing but oatmeal, juices, soups and milk shakes. And he refused weekend passes, because he didn't want his widowed mother to see her youngest son unable to laugh. His family laughed a lot. Francis felt that once he received his false teeth he would go home. But when he had them installed, he refused his weekend pass again, remaining in the barracks, sulking. All week long he avoided people, trying hard to hide his face. One night I confronted him and coerced him to look at me. He was grotesque. Francis had been fitted with the biggest teeth I had ever seen in a human being's head. Why, they were so big he couldn't close his lips. Because he wasn't a complainer, he was willing to live with the teeth. At first he balked when I insisted he ask the company commander to approach the chief base dentist for a more natural looking set of teeth. I practically had to drag Francis to the captain's office. Two weeks later he went home to see his mother.

CHAPTER
THREE

Encouraging Confidence and Self-Esteem

Little did I know that while working as a journalist, I was preparing myself for a career in education. I spent fifteen years in journalism, working for newspapers and radio and television stations and networks. Even while teaching, I wrote public affairs articles for a leading New England magazine, and still take on freelance assignments.

When I left DePauw, I wasn't thinking of journalism as a career. I seriously thought of attending law school at night, but changed my mind when a friend's father got me a job with the New York *Journal American*, a conservative Hearst owned newspaper that is now defunct. It was nothing glamorous. Starting as a copy boy, I ran far more errands than wrote copy. My most memorable assignment was writing captions for a photographer covering the 1953 baseball World Series, between the Brooklyn Dodgers and the New York Yankees. Before the first game started at Ebbets Field, I remember peering down from the press box at the playing field and recalling the day I worked out there as an aspiring professional baseball player who couldn't distinguish between an adverbial clause and a prepositional phrase.

It was thrilling seeing my copy printed in a New York City newspaper, even if it was only captions. My mother made sure that everyone she knew on our block saw the five or six sentences I had written.

My stay at the *Journal American* was short-lived; not because I didn't like what I was doing. Oh I could have done less errands and more writing, but that was okay, for I liked the excitement of the newsroom, and there was promise of promotion to reporter. While at the newspaper I discovered what I wanted to do professionally. That was a big breakthrough in my life, for there would be no more agonizing over what profession I would pursue. I was focused on journalism — me, the guy whose worst subject in school was English.

The Army pulled me away from the *Journal American*, but it had no effect on my new focus. I was determined to turn the two years in the military into a journalism experience. At Fort Dix I tried to land a job as a reporter for the base newspaper, but I didn't get it. And it wasn't for lack of trying on my part. During the first month of basic training I spent most of my free time at the newspaper office, volunteering my services. I even wrote several articles that were published. The editor's official reason for not hiring me was the lack of openings. But I knew from staff members that he was looking to expand his reporter corps. I guess he didn't like my writing style — or last name.

For some reason I knew there would be other journalistic opportunities in the Army. One came my way while at Fort Dix, something that would never have been endorsed by the base hierarchy, and certainly never reported by the base newspaper. It was a whopper of a story, that had national implications. I was so excited that I never thought of what could happen to me if I were caught covering a story that could get the Fort Dix Commanding General in trouble. To me it was a great adventure. It was also an opportunity to expose a gross injustice, and the fact that pursuing the story could help me make important contacts with the New York press corps didn't escape me.

G. David Schine, a special investigator for the late Senator Joseph McCarthy, was receiving preferential treatment from the Fort Dix Commanding General. It riled me to see the general's limousine come for Schine while the rest of us were doing kitchen patrol or mopping the barracks floor.

I knew I had a good story. And the fact that Schine was in my squad and slept in the next bunk made my job as an unofficial reporter fairly easy. I watched every move he made, making note of every time the general's limousine called for him, every time he missed bivouacs or long battle dress treks into the woods. When I felt I had enough information for a legitimate news story, I contacted the *New York Post*, in those days one of the most liberal newspapers in America. I didn't consider contacting the *Journal American*, because it supported many of Senator McCarthy's positions. My pipeline to the outside world was *Post* reporter Irving Leiberman. I would call him from pay-phone booths, or meet him in different Manhattan restaurants while on a weekend pass.

When the *Post* published the story, our company was rife with rumor and speculation as to how the newspaper got its information. The sergeant said, "It had to be an inside job." I remained tight-lipped and scared, for I finally realized that if I were caught, the general would ship me to Korea as a rifleman on the first available plane.

The preferential treatment for Schine stopped. While that was the source of some personal satisfaction, it meant the end of my self-generated "cloak and dagger" journalistic enterprise. The excitement was over, and I was faced with trying to concoct a way to avoid being shipped overseas as a rifleman. Since basic training would be completed in ten days, I didn't have much time to successfully wangle a non-combatant assignment, as some of the other draftees did. My frantic attempt failed. Getting my shipping orders was like getting my death notice. I was to be shipped to Fort Lewis in Washington state, to await further assignment to the Far East as an infantryman. I was sure I was headed for Korea. It didn't matter that a truce had been arranged. Shooting could resume any time, I thought.

But I got a break. I didn't leave Fort Dix when everyone else in my company shipped out. Somehow the Army learned of my role in exposing the preferential treatment Schine had received. I was being held behind to possibly testify in the Senate Army-McCarthy hearings, as a witness for the Army.

While I never testified, it felt good to know that my unofficial journalistic enterprise during basic training was a factor in holding the hearings, which, in turn, led to Senator McCarthy's political demise.

The rest of my Army career was spent in Okinawa.

While in the Army I couldn't appreciate how the Schine affair furthered my understanding of how humans learn, but now I do. While covering Schine, I was extremely alert, because I understood what my mission was and what good could result from it. In school, my teachers never explained why it was important to learn to read, write and do arithmetic. You did what the teacher said you had to do, relying on a dull textbook to get his points across. Later on, when I had the opportunity to teach, I instinctively shared with students why they had to learn certain material and how it would benefit them. With that kind of vision most students are motivated to learn, for they have a better idea of why they are in school. School becomes an essential building block to their future; it becomes an adventure, an exciting challenge instead of a meaningless duty.

In my first television news job, I didn't know how to write for film. It's very different from writing for a newspaper. I had a vision of succeeding, and I liked what I saw, and that motivated me to learn what I needed to know. First, I mapped out a strategy on how I was going to implement my vision. On my own time, I studied my co-workers' scripts, studied film clips, asked my colleagues questions. In about three weeks my TV news writing was as good as the others on the staff.

Some might argue that fear of losing my job was the prime motivator in learning to write for film. Perhaps that was a subconscious factor, but I know it wasn't the overriding reason. If fear were the primary reason, I would have quit the job, creating plausible excuses as to why I had done the right thing by quitting. On the other hand, I knew I needed help in keeping focused on the vision, because I had a tendency to abandon projects I sensed I was incapable of carrying out. I couldn't stand failing. Prayer kept me focused.

I learned other things about education from my journalism experiences. For example, there is more than one way of doing things right. I know many traditional educators would reject that notion, but personal experience has shown me that they need to remove the fog from their glasses.

When I landed a job as producer of the Eleventh Hour news for a Philadelphia TV station, the news director insisted I follow, to the letter, the producing procedures of the person I was replacing. For a week I struggled to emulate my predecessor's approaches and methods. I was failing, and he knew it, and so did the news director. My job was in jeopardy. Only I knew I could do what had to be done; but I couldn't do it the way the news director wanted it done. Both he and the person I was replacing were very methodical in their approach and exceedingly analytical. I was more instinctive and creative. Compounding the problem was our different television journalism philosophies. The fact that I found the outgoing producer abrasive and rigid in his thinking was also a problem; he reminded me of some of my school teachers. In desperation, I went to the newscaster, who was more flexible, and asked if he would allow me to employ my producing approach for a week. He had no objections.

It worked. In fact, in less than a year, we were able to turn a last- rated newscast into the top-rated newscast in the region.

Through journalism I learned to persevere, a quality a scholar also needs to succeed. While a journalist's deadlines are usually far more pressing than a scholar's, to do a credible job he must persist in unearthing all of the facts, the obvious as well as the hidden.

There were times while working on an investigative assignment in Minneapolis when I seriously thought of abandoning the project, especially when I learned that my family's wellbeing was at stake. The investigation was hatched during an interview I did with an Eisenhower Administration official. He suggested I explore the background of the leader of the biggest labor union in Minneapolis. I followed his advice. While it was tedious work, every time I made a breakthrough my resolve to complete the probe was quickened. It was like putting a puzzle together, except the puzzle dealt with humans, some of whom were dangerous.

The union leader was a former member of the Purple Gang, a Midwestern rival of the Al Capone mob. After more checking, I learned that he and a local insurance company, headed by a former FBI chief of the upper Midwest, had concocted a medical insurance scheme for the workers of a large, locally based corporation. For his efforts, the union leader received hefty kickbacks from the insurance company head.

There were other revelations. The labor big-shot had close connections with a leading restaurateur and part-owner of a professional basketball team, who turned out to be an important underworld figure with strong political ties in Washington.

I didn't mind the hundreds of telephone calls I had to make, and scores of people I had to interview, because from some of those efforts I was able to obtain leads that would produce another piece to the puzzle. What I minded was the dangerous situation I found myself in. Strange-looking characters were following me on the street. There were threatening phone calls. The first and last time I met the person I was investigating was in the lobby of Minneapolis City Hall, my normal beat. He and two of his henchmen approached me. At the time I wondered how he was able to identify me. (Of course, that was before I became aware that I was being trailed.) The man was blunt: "You'll get into trouble, Sonny, if you don't stop what you're doing."

I sent my wife and 14-month-old son back East to stay with my in-laws. Before heading for work every day I would check underneath my car to see if any odd-looking objects had been planted there.

After the man I was investigating died of a heart attack, I left Minneapolis, thinking that I was ready, after only a year's experience, to be a network correspondent. At the time, I would never have admitted that I left for New York to avoid being killed.

While deeply involved with the probe, I had no idea of how my perseverance was helping me acquire essential educational skills, skills I had never learned in school. Namely, how to collect data and collate it; how to unearth evidence and appraise it; how to identify meaningful sources and sift meaningful information from them; and how to budget one's time and energy. It was the challenge itself that forced me to appreciate and master those principles. Had those principles been introduced to me via a lecture in a classroom I would have brushed them aside as meaningless abstractions. Now as an educator I value those principles highly, and have organized situations in class whereby students have an opportunity to discover and internalize them. Their challenges arise from simulated real-life projects.

Years later, while working for NBC News, I conquered a certain journalistic challenge that proved to me that I could do what I always felt I couldn't do. I despised dealing with details. To this day I become anxious when filling out a form. I've always considered myself an ideas person, more intuitive than rational, someone who thinks in pictures instead of words. Psychologists would classify me as a "right-hemisphere brain" person, one who communicates more effectively through images than words, who thinks holistically, is more intuitive than logical.

In my second month as a news editor, I found myself battling my toughest professional test. I had to plan and produce coverage of the America's Cup for audiences in four continents. I never had trouble generating story ideas and covering them with style so they would be easily understood by the viewer. But charting a week-long campaign on a topic I had no interest in and knew nothing about was, I felt, an impossible undertaking for me. I wanted desperately to wangle out of the assignment. Why choose me, I thought, when there were at least two guys in the newsroom who were yachting enthusiasts. But reason didn't prevail. I had to do it.

Before I could start working on the plan, I had to do a self-directed cram course on yachting, yacht racing and the history of the America's Cup. Familiarizing myself with the competing Australian and American yachts and their crews also had to be done.

Shaping the plan was like shaping a big military campaign. Billeting had to be found in two cities for the four film crews, production assistants, a film editing crew and couriers that I had to organize and coordinate; a plane and boat had to be rented for sea level and air shots; a helicopter and motorcycle courier service had to be rented to transport our footage 75 miles to a film processing lab that had to be close to the television station where we edited and wrote and fed our completed stories to our audiences via communications satellite. All of the overseas feeds had to be booked through Comsat, taking into account the different time zones.

In putting the plan together I had to anticipate whatever logistical, production, editorial, or personnel problems could possibly arise. For example, to ensure that our footage wouldn't be lost at sea, I had to order special bright orange floatable casings for the cans of film that were to be picked up by helicopter in open sea off Newport, Rhode Island and flown to Boston for processing. Of course the plan had to reflect some solid cost consciousness, too.

Fortunately, we encountered no serious difficulties during the coverage period. Everything went according to plan. While all of our audiences were happy with our feeds, I don't think anyone in the world was happier than me. It wasn't the praise from my fellow journalists that moved me. What moved me was knowing that I had done something I once believed I was incapable of doing. I had developed some of the left hemisphere of my brain which, I suspect, had been dormant for years, probably since doing high school mathematics. For the next four years that part of my brain must have experienced further development, for I had to organize many other big news campaigns. It seems the more planning I did the better planner I became. In fact, in time, I looked forward to organizing the next big news coverage campaign.

Interestingly, those experiences influenced my attitude toward teaching. In my classes today, students strike from their mind and vocabulary the term "can't do." They may find an assignment or project difficult, but they know they are capable of doing it; and when they do it, they gain confidence, a quality that's necessary for intellectual growth. Of course, though they all do it there are quality differences; not every result is exactly alike.

CHAPTER
FOUR

Understanding Human Potential

I never thought of being a teacher. In fact, I never dreamt of being involved in any phase of formal education, mainly because I didn't think I was capable of doing it, nor worthy of such a high calling. Yet I ended up teaching.

Most men and women with fifteen years' experience in a field they enjoy, and making steady professional headway, wouldn't enter a new profession, especially one they had never trained for. For a while when people asked why I left NBC News in the prime of my professional years to teach in Amherst, Massachusetts, I would usually say that my wife and I wanted to leave the frenetic metropolitan New York City area, that we were looking for a healthier social setting for our children. But those weren't the real reasons, although our children did benefit from our move to rural New England.

Actually, I think there were two reasons I made the switch. One wasn't easily discernible. It had to do with revenge. Subconsciously, I had a need to get back at an educational system that I believed failed me, and many others like me, and even those who graduated with honors, for we were all deprived of something essential, which I'll touch on later in this book. The other reason, the more apparent one, had to do with human magnetism. I was persuaded, in part, to make the change by an innovative, flamboyant educator who could sell electric room heaters to Sahara nomads. Dr. Dwight Allen, Dean of the University of Massachusetts School of Education, came to NBC News to be interviewed by Barbara Walters on a program called Not for Women Only. Before the interview, Allen combed the newsroom looking for me, but I wasn't around. He wanted to talk to me about a magazine article I had written regarding the future of television journalism. As a futurist, he found my vision intriguing. After his taping session, he returned to the newsroom and found me at my desk talking to a photographer in the Dominican Republic.

Allen seemed like a patient man, for he waited at least ten minutes before I could talk to him.

"Do you have fifteen minutes to spare?" he said.

I checked my watch. "I think so."

We ended up in a coffee shop in the building where our news department was housed. I never finished my coffee, because Allen's adventurist spirit was overwhelming. He wanted me to head a doctorate degree-offering department in his school. It didn't matter that I didn't even have a Masters Degree. Every reason I gave why I couldn't make the move, he overruled. For example, when I told him I couldn't afford a pay cut, he offered me more money than I was making.

I later learned that Allen was a very intuitive person. When he felt he was right, he went after it, regardless of long established traditions, protocol and carefully reasoned advice from colleagues.

I guess after speaking to me for five minutes he felt we were kindred spirits. He was an educational revolutionary with a Ph.D. from Stanford; and I was a victim of the system he wanted to change, someone who wanted to see the system altered, too. He probably sensed that I was — like him — a natural iconoclast who thrived on taking risks for just causes.

The three years I taught at the University of Massachusetts as one of the highest paid lecturers in the school's history, was an enriching experience for me, perhaps even more so than for my students. Not that everything went smoothly: it didn't. The tests made me grow. In many ways it was a humbling experience, because as a non-academic in a high-powered academic institution, I quickly became aware of how ill-equipped I was to help undergraduate students to graduate, not to mention the ten doctoral students who chose me to guide them toward earning their degrees.

Fortunately, I learned fast. Drawing upon my highly developed "street smarts," I was able to organize and teach courses, as well as properly assist the postgraduate students. It was a fascinating situation, because by helping the students I found myself in an unofficial doctoral-level crash course. I guess there is some truth to the adage that in teaching a course the teacher learns more than the pupils. After a year at the university, I knew how to negotiate the academic infrastructure, and confidently chair a doctoral dissertation committee.

While I had survived my test as a teacher, I didn't fare well as chairman of my department. Pressured to secure grants for research and development projects, I expended a great deal of energy and time in producing proposals and calling on foundations and public agencies for funding. All I could manage was one small grant. Resigning as chairman was a relief.

No longer haunted by the need to secure grants, I was able to reflect clearly on my career and interest goals. I was astounded by the clarity of the first idea that came to mind: write a book about television's influence on children. What amazed me was my confidence to do it. It didn't matter that I hadn't written one before. I had the tools and conditions to do it, I reasoned: I had a strong working knowledge of television, and yearning to know more of how children learn and what shapes their behavior. The university's research facilities were excellent, and since I was free of the chairmanship burden, I had the time and peace of mind to write the book. The fact that I enjoyed writing also figured in my decision to start the project. The fact that the title came to me before I had thought of an outline was a good sign. "Go Watch TV" is a term used by parents to get rid of their children while doing chores, or needing some time alone.

To spur me on, I organized a course on the impact of television on children, which turned out to be the first draft of the book's outline. Only fifteen students took the course, but among them was a noted university researcher in child psychology, Dr. Dan Anderson. Both he and his top graduate assistant had a keen interest in how TV impacts on children.

During the next eighteen months we developed a close relationship. He shared most of his research findings with me and introduced me to the meaningful child psychology literature. And the discussions we had over lunch, in his lab or my office were also helpful. Despite my difficulty with reading, I pored over the material I received from Dan. It wasn't easy, for I had to plod through bogs of academic jargon. But it was worth it — the stuff helped to provide the book with substance.

Dan profited from our relationship as well. He gained an inside view of how television operates in America, plus the questions raised in my class moved him to organize new research ventures. I also introduced him to my contacts at *Sesame Street's* research department, which led to his developing a long working association with them.

It was a good time. I was making steady headway in completing my first book. And I was growing intellectually. It was more than the research I was engaged in, and the stimulating discussions with Dan Anderson and his associates, that generated the growth. Being alone and having the time to focus on issues that had become important to me helped me to discover aspects of reality I had never known before. But what I had discovered — though important — wasn't as meaningful to me as how I gained the insights. It was like a child who had been walking for months, suddenly learning how to run. Focused deep thinking for a relatively long period of time, like 30 or 40 minutes, was a new experience. Most of my life I had been an improvisational thinker, using whatever intelligence I had at the time to react to on-the-spot demands and challenges at school, work and play. Even in journalism there usually wasn't much time to make decisions, or enough time to cover a story thoroughly. As an editor I learned to deal with those conditions, as well as learning to handle a number of equally important tasks at once. Certainly a valuable ability, but not as satisfying for me as what I gained from meditating on a problem or issue. The light of understanding that broke through the darkness of doubt thrilled me.

I had such an experience pondering the nature of education. It was a simple message: check out the Bahá'í view. I did, and was struck by a particular passage I had read numerous times in the past, but had never pondered:

> Regard man [female and male] as a mine rich in gems of inestimable value. Education can, alone, cause it to reveal its treasures, and enable mankind to benefit therefrom.*

It was an eye-opener. I had never linked personal discovery with education. I, like the rest of my colleagues, friends and relatives, believed that education was the drilling of knowledge into students' heads. That certainly had been my experience in elementary school, high school, even college. And at the School of Education most pedagogists were busy refining and reforming the accepted basis of educating humans. With my new understanding, what was being done in our schools no longer made sense. Worse than that, children and youth were being cheated, some even psychologically crippled. And tragically, most educators weren't aware of the damage they were doing to the human beings they were charged with helping to grow intellectually and emotionally. Educators were going in the wrong direction. Instead of continually pushing in information, they should have been spending a good portion of their classroom time drawing out those "gems of inestimable value" in children.

As for those gems within us all, they represent our human potential, I reasoned. And human potential consisted of the talents and capacities and moral attributes in all of us. No teacher, with the exception of Mrs. Fleming, ever tried to draw out my potential, help me understand what it was, and provide guidance on how to develop it, and how to use it when developed.

At the highly toted school of education where I worked, prospective teachers weren't being trained to discover, release and develop human potential. They still aren't, and I doubt if any other American school of education is doing it today.

*Gleanings from the Writings of Bahá'u'lláh, pp. 259-60

As I pondered what I had discovered, I realized how the drawing out process can create in students, regardless of economic and social standing, skin color, religion, or ethnic origin, a sense of self-worth and confidence. Discovering your potential, even some of it, can also generate a sense of wonderment, making life exciting, full of hope.

By discovering his potential, a child begins to understand who he is, something that most children and adults today have little or no knowledge of. Because they lack such knowledge, they allow themselves to be fashioned by all of the ugly stimuli they are exposed to daily. They move through life ignorant of who they really are, adopting the ways of their media and sports heroes and what advertisements dictate as the accepted attitudes and behavior for the moment. The good and beauty within them remains dormant. Unaware of their true selves, they become slaves to convention. I can think of no greater waste than that.

While becoming acquainted with his potential strengthens a student emotionally, it also provides him with an awareness of his talents and interests, ingredients needed to weave a vision of his future career. The vision provides him with something meaningful to aim for, and helps him establish order and security in his life. Without vision a person gropes for something to do professionally, and in the process is usually plagued by anxiety, often settling for a job he doesn't like, causing an unhappiness that affects all other aspects of his life.

As I pondered the nature of education, it became clear that a teacher had two major responsibilities: discovering and developing students' human potential, and teaching learning skills, the former being the more important, for a math whiz lacking self-esteem, confidence, and vision of what course he should take in life will most likely end up anxious, confused, frustrated and fearful of the future.

Only one of the school of education's departments shared that view. The Anisa Project was committed to creating a theoretical base for the discovery and development of human potential. With only one professor and about 20 graduate students, the department had little political clout in the school.

In fact, it was the object of scorn and jokes by the bigger and better funded departments. Academic critics had difficulty accepting the spiritual dimension of Anisa's theory. So did most of the funding agencies. To me it made sense to develop a human being's spiritual nature and body as well as his mind.

I read Anisa's literature, befriended some of its students, probably the brightest, most open-minded, ethical, idealistic students in the school. Several of them asked me to serve on their doctoral dissertation committees.

By the time I left the University of Massachusetts I had formed a view of education. It wasn't a complete philosophy, nor was it scientifically tested. It was a belief based on a spiritual teaching, and as far as I knew it hadn't been tried. Of course, the thought of becoming another fanatical faculty member hawking another educational "panacea" didn't escape me. Consequently, I didn't try to convert anyone to my view, but I did discuss it with some Anisa staff members, hoping to gain new insights. And I did.

Ironically, I left the university better prepared to teach on a college level than when I arrived. But my chances of applying what I had figured out were extremely slim, for I was fed up with academic life. It wasn't teaching classes that bothered me. Actually, I enjoyed working with students. It was the campus politics that I couldn't take.

The experience that convinced me that I was in the wrong profession occurred across campus. I belonged to the University Broadcasting Council, a body composed of several Communication Department professors at the College of Arts and Sciences, the College of Engineering's Associate Dean, the General Manager of the 30,000 watt NPR-affiliated university radio station, and a representative from the School of Business Administration. The Radio General Manager and myself were the only ones with broadcasting experience.

When we received news from the Federal Communications Commission that the university had been awarded a license to operate a UHF TV station, I was ecstatic. But no one else shared my enthusiasm. At first, I was baffled. How could they oppose such an opportunity, I wondered. All of the benefits of having a television station on campus flashed through my mind: it wouldn't only be an outlet for the Public Broadcasting Service's fine programming for the people living in the Amherst area; lectures, recitals, concerts, drama and thought-provoking workshops produced at the university could be aired, enriching not only the students and faculty but the community-at-large; and Communication majors, as well as students pursuing other disciplines, would have a first-class laboratory to sharpen their broadcasting skills and be exposed to professional realities. I was so enthusiastic about the idea I drafted a detailed programming proposal, and a plan outlining how the Arts and Sciences Communication Department should reorganize itself to make the best use of the TV facility; I even listed and described possible course offerings.

I was shocked when the Council rejected the FCC's offer. On the surface, the reasons for the negative decision seemed plausible: operating a station would detract from the faculty's attention to their students and research; involvement in a broadcasting enterprise would promote professionalism instead of scholarship; and securing funding to set up and maintain the facility would be an added hardship for the administration.

My counter arguments didn't even dent the barrier the other Council members had erected between them and me. In a few days — after considerable reflection and campus probing — it became apparent why the other Council members turned down the offer: the Communications Department members were afraid of exposing their ignorance of "hands-on" professional TV operations; the other members had a deepseated fear of change, especially when it had to do with a technology they had very little knowledge of. And the radio manager feared that a TV station would divert interest and funding from the station he headed. To me it was another example of academics putting their own interests ahead of their students.

I left the University of Massachusetts disillusioned with higher education, my original image of academe shattered. I had always thought of my colleagues as bastions of integrity, free of the clawing for power, character assassination, backbiting, lying, plagiarism, jealousy and envy that characterized the corporate world. But I was wrong. In fact, the social climate at the University of Massachusetts was worse than any corporate experience I ever had in my professional life. It was the pretense of integrity that made it worse. At least in the corporate world employees, rank and file and management, expect and adjust to the "survival of the fittest" atmosphere. I know now that I was terribly naive when I first stepped onto the campus.

Three years later I was a lot wiser, not only about the internal workings of a university and all of its intrigues, but I had benefited intellectually from the experience. By discovering more of my potential, I grew to understand more about myself; and my outlook was certainly broadened. I was familiar with theories and philosophies I had never encountered before, which stimulated some deep thinking. It was also a humbling experience. Being stripped of my chairmanship helped me to straighten out my priorities in life: serving others was more important than wielding power.

I also came to the conclusion that the University of Massachusetts' School of Education, with all of its dynamism, was incapable of creating an educational model that would effectively replace the failing school systems of America. Its pedagogists were so immersed in the prevailing pedagogical ways, so comfortable with their professional situations, especially the tenured faculty, that deep down they feared radical change. And radical change was and still is required.

CHAPTER
FIVE

The Teacher as Servant

Though I left the university, my wife and I decided to remain in Amherst. Our children were thriving there; life was pleasant and the countryside beautiful; we had good friends, and I was able to earn a living in the area freelancing. Sheed and Ward Publishing's decision to publish my book was also a factor in my not moving. Little did I know at the time that one of my consultancies would lead to a permanent job, a job that would turn out to be the most rewarding and professionally gratifying experience of my life.

Had someone told me at the time that I would end up staying at Springfield Technical Community College for the next fifteen years I would have laughed in his face. For during my university experience I had been influenced by many of my former colleagues' low opinion of community colleges. I couldn't see myself working in a glorified vocational school for the rest of my life.

The college hired me as a temporary consultant to teach its teachers to teach on television. It was planning to offer courses through the local public TV station. Shortly before completion of the teaching project, STCC's Academic Dean, John Dunn, asked me to draft a curriculum for a television communications program, which the college wanted to start in the fall. I did it.

And in mid-May I went to New York City to spend the summer working as a news writer for NBC's *Today* program. While it was exciting being involved in big time journalism again, especially during the peak of the Watergate scandal, I knew I could never live in the New York area again. By nine a.m. Friday, the end of the last *Today* program of the week, I was itching to head for the clear skies and open spaces of Amherst. It was good to know that after the last Friday in August I would be home and wouldn't have to drive back to mid-Manhattan late Sunday night again.

I left the *Today* program about two weeks earlier than I had planned, because of a phone call I received in early June from John Dunn, as I was leaving the newsroom for a weekend in Amherst. He asked if I would organize and head a television communications department at his school. I was startled, because I had not expected the offer. The idea of teaching and heading a department again scared me. The wounds I had sustained at the University of Massachusetts were still fresh; and there was the vow I had made that I would never teach on a college level again; and I was also plagued by the idea that someone with my qualifications and experience should be working in a far more prestigious and challenging place than a community college. I needed time to think it over and consult with my wife. I knew that she would feel more secure if I had a permanent job with practical benefits like medical and life insurance. But I liked freelancing, because I was my own boss, I could set my own agenda, set my own pace, and do what I wanted to do best. I had had my fill of college committees and campus intrigues. When Dean Dunn offered to speak to me that afternoon, I accepted the invitation, hoping our consultation would provide me with clearer focus.

It was a good meeting. He was enthusiastic about the prospect of me teaching at STCC, yet he didn't try to sell me on the college, or try to coerce me to take the job. He said he was impressed with the curriculum I had prepared and was attuned to my educational philosophy. That impressed me. So did his commitment to helping students. Not a word was mentioned about securing "soft money" grants, or my having to organize a departmental governance body, or having to serve on committees. The primary emphasis at STCC was in serving students, helping them grow intellectually and helping them develop a marketable skill. He assured me that if I took the job, neither he nor anyone else on campus would interfere with my program as long as it served the students well. He also promised to provide our department with the equipment needed to make our program top notch.

Though I took the job, I wasn't committed to staying long — a year or two, tops. For while Dean Dunn seemed sincere, I was still suspicious of college administrators and felt uneasy interacting with academic types. What I really wanted to do was write books and produce television documentaries. My secret hope was that after a short stint at STCC, I would be able to support my family by doing those things.

But I remained at the community college, despite good job offers from other places. After my first semester, I began to sense that I was working where I belonged. I actually looked forward to going to work in the morning, even though it was a 27-mile trip to Springfield. In a short time, I had developed a strong rapport with the students whose attitude was very different from those I served at the university. They weren't consumed by political fervor, with a passion to remake the world according to their blurred utopian view. Most of them were first generation college men and women, from working class families, with little confidence regarding their academic ability. It was an ethnically diverse group, with eighteen-year-olds in the same classroom with grandmothers on Welfare. What impressed me was that despite their differences, they were all serious about their studies, even those who were struggling to keep pace with those who had stronger educational backgrounds; and the fact that most of them held jobs while going to school moved me. I was amazed that they were able to find the time and energy to do their homework assignments. I really wanted to help them; and they knew it. I suspect my empathy stemmed from equating my school experiences as a youth with theirs.

At the end of the academic year I felt good about what I had experienced at STCC. I had seen people grow intellectually, gain confidence and a broader view of life. Their apprehension regarding formal education had evaporated. In fact, at least 75% of them wanted to pursue a Bachelor's Degree after completing the television communications program. And that's what they did. It was an amazing transformation, for the great majority of the students had entered our program to learn a marketable skill in two years and then find a decent job. Spending another two years in school was out of the question.

My decision to stay at Springfield Technical Community College was made the second year there, at the graduation commencement exercises. It was more than seeing our first graduates receiving their Associate Degrees, something they probably thought they would never get while floundering in high school, or hanging around on their neighborhood street corners. It was an experience I had with one of the graduates and his parents immediately after the commencement that convinced me to stay.

It was a hot, steamy day, and I was about to step out of my gown and dash to my air-conditioned car, when Peter Jourdain, one of our top graduates, ran up to me, asking that I meet his parents who were waiting under a big shade tree across the campus green.

The parents were simple people, who had never graduated from high school. The father, who was an unskilled laborer, was unemployed at the time, and I doubt if his wife had a job. But on that day you would never have known their true economic and social condition; they were in their best clothes, dressed like they were at a wedding.

Peter was the first of their eight children to attend college. When I shook the father's hand, he and his wife began to cry. Peter's eyes were teary, and I cried. We spent the next few minutes hugging each other. Though little was said, it was one of the most heart-pleasing conversations I have ever had.

Peter's parents knew that their son had a rebirth experience at STCC — a rebirth, and not simply a second chance, because Peter discovered a part of himself he had never known before. What he discovered was good, very good: he was bright, creative, possessing a rich curiosity that spawned an insatiable hunger for

knowledge. The schools he attended before were unaware of
those qualities. To them, Peter was a poor student, a trouble-
maker, who would end up like most of the other youths in his
tough Holyoke neighborhood, working in a mill or with a road
construction crew — and that's if he was lucky.

All the way home I could think of nothing else but Peter and
his parents and our embrace. I reviewed my relationship with
Peter over the past two years. In a way, I thought, it was a
miracle that the guy graduated with top honors. For the first
month at STCC, he seemed to be a tall, lanky, undisciplined,
unfocused nineteen-year-old whose primary reason for being in
college was to play hockey and baseball and have a "good time."
He couldn't even write a simple sentence correctly.

It would have been easy to have branded him an ineducable
type, and allowed him to drift toward dropping out. I can
understand why many teachers with large classes do that sort of
thing. It is a way of reducing job pressure. But I couldn't do it,
especially after discovering in Peter's writing what Mrs. Fleming
discovered in mine. When I shared with him that he had the
potential to be a writer, something clicked within him. That
dazed look on his face disappeared; his eyes were alive with
curiosity — and hope. We spent a long time talking in my
office. I pointed out how he could develop his potential — and
he did it, finding time to do it despite his normal school load, a
job and hockey practice and games. He would get up at five a.m.
every morning to write in his journal for an hour. Because
someone he respected believed in him, and he had a vision of
what the exercise would do for him, he was willing to make the
sacrifice. In time, getting up early was no longer a hardship,
because there was joy in experiencing growth and making
progress in achieving a goal.

Peter's appetite for knowledge increased. After graduating
with top honors, he was awarded a scholarship to Syracuse
University where he excelled as a broadcast journalism major.

But his education didn't end there. Deciding to become a
lawyer instead of a journalist, he was admitted into the
University of Michigan Law School, one of the best law schools
in America. In his first year he was cited as one of the ten top

writers in his class, a class made up of young men and women who did their undergraduate work at places like Harvard and Yale. He worked two years as a communications lawyer for a firm in Ann Arbor when a powerful urge to further his education drove him to accept a fellowship from Harvard University to do a Ph.D. in English Literature.

During the summer following the graduation of our first class, I started searching for answers as to why so many students benefited, in a profound way, from our program. I had to find out, because the results mystified me. I certainly didn't anticipate those results. It just happened. But how could that be? I thought. Doesn't every effect have a cause?

Actually, what resulted was a surprise that thrust upon me new challenges. One in particular stood out: I had an incredible opportunity to serve men and women who were earnestly reaching out for ways of overcoming a condition of hopelessness. To witness intellectual and spiritual growth, especially in men and women who had always felt inadequate, was like seeing and feeling the sun after weeks of incessant rain. And to know that I played a role in my students finding light in their lives generated within me a feeling that a life guard must feel when he saves a drowning child. You become acquainted with your inherent goodness, and you want to do more good.

I went about my inquiry like a miner who had stumbled upon a few scattered diamonds at the base of a worn and weathered hill. Why did my students respond to me the way they did when I had no formal training as a teacher? I had never taken an education course in college; and what I had done in the classroom at the University of Massachusetts would have horrified most college accreditation evaluators. I had relied on a combination of intuition, street smarts, my past professional experience in the communications field, my understanding of what a human being is — and prayer. My approach at STCC was no different. (I have never organized a lesson plan in the 21 years I have taught in college.)

Since I was baffled over my success at STCC, I couldn't announce that I had discovered an innovative way of teaching;

nor could I well up with pride over successfully executing a brilliant plan I had devised. There was no plan. Then was it a fluke? An accident? No, because the second year of the program was more effective than the first year. Even after I began to realize why I had been successful, I was hesitant to take credit, because I wasn't certain that what I was doing would be acceptable to the administration. My teaching approach was antithetical to established educational procedures. There were times when I would say to myself: "Let's face it — you're winging it. You're too lazy to prepare a lesson plan." And I would counter with, "But a lesson plan would inhibit me, kill the spontaneity of my approach, keep me from addressing those students' questions and problems that the plan wasn't designed to address."

My inner dialogue continued for a number of years. There were even times when I considered myself an academic fraud. That feeling usually surfaced when I attended educational conferences that had to do with staff and curriculum development. Speaker after speaker, often employing carefully crafted flow charts, spoke, like dispassionate surgeons describing intricate surgical procedures, about esoteric pedagogical subjects I had difficulty grasping. In time I understood why I had such difficulty: I had instinctively blocked out what was being said because the speakers were treating teaching as a technology and students like consumers devoid of spirit. What they talked about wasn't applicable to what I was doing. I had to teach the only way I knew how.

To me teaching is an act of service. Therefore, as a teacher I consider myself a servant, a term many of my colleagues feel belittles their profession. I feel as a teacher I have a highly sensitive responsibility to help human beings not only learn a marketable skill, but more important, discover their intellectual and character strengths and weaknesses. By doing the latter my students become acquainted with who they are and develop an understanding of what they have to do to fulfill their potential and become a human being who has a dynamic grasp of the purpose of life.

They know I care, and are aware that in our classes they are receiving something they don't expect from a school, namely, direction in their lives. It is more than career counseling; it has to do with becoming stronger within, more confident, better focused and a more compassionate human being.

Of course my classroom approach isn't immediately embraced by the students. At first I feel rejected; but in time it becomes apparent why they're hesitant to accept me as a legitimate teacher. They have been conditioned by previous school experiences to expect textbook assignments, quizzes, and teachers who avoid involvement in students' personal problems. I'm different, even bizarre to some; but I feel I have to do what's right even if it runs counter to established educational custom. I purposely get involved in my students' lives, even their problems outside of school. I do it despite the advice of colleagues not to. They're afraid that by counseling students I make myself vulnerable to legal action. Advising men and women about life, they feel, should be left to licensed counselors. I know the warning was given with my best interest at heart, but had I heeded it, many of my students would have been detoured permanently from reaching their important goals. To be an effective teacher, I feel, you have to be willing to take risks. Often, I have discovered, a student's poor performance can be traced to his emotional make-up, a problem at home, or an unfortunate school experience in his past. (More about risk-taking later in the book.)

I make it a policy to warn all incoming students about my unorthodox approach. Nevertheless, for the first few weeks they are cautious, some slightly bewildered, but interestingly, very few drop out. A sense of intrigue and a burning curiosity keeps them in the program, I guess. Usually by the third week they are settled in — and a bonding starts to develop between us, the kind of bonding that develops among family members. To enhance the feeling of oneness I never hesitate giving my address or phone number to those students who ask for them. Many a problem has been solved through a phone call after school hours — sometimes after midnight.

But the class song is the major factor in reinforcing a spirit of family in our program. It's a mindless song, something not even the producers of *Monty Python* would allow on their television show. For example, one of them is an exaggerated British version of the theme song of the old American Davey Crockett TV show. It goes like this:

> "Dye-vee, Dye-vee Crotchet
> Regis of the wooly fron-tee-ya
> Ee-ya, ee-ya, ee-ya."

To do it right, considerable vibrato is required in the last line. By the time they graduate most students have mastered the requirement. The class song is sung almost every time we assemble in the classroom. In fact, singing the song at graduation commencement exercises has become an unofficial college tradition. After the more than 5,000 students, guests and dignitaries are seated in the Springfield Civic Center, and the first speaker starts speaking, our graduates arise, and with great gusto bellow forth their song — sparking applause from the crowd. Though in time most students find singing the song a fun experience, it takes on a more profound meaning, especially for the older students who have a history of doing poorly in school. For them it signifies a new day, one that's pregnant with hope. They're purging themselves of the pain spawned in the past; and maybe for the first time in their lives, they're looking at the future with some confidence. They usually sing the song with such feeling that when they conclude singing, students in adjoining classrooms often break out in applause. A popular radio show, doing a remote broadcast from our college, heard about the song and had us do it live over the air waves.

Frankly, I'm amazed how attached my students are to their class song, even those with high SAT scores, who at first find singing in class an embarrassment. Its significance in their lives became most apparent to me at a funeral service for a young woman who had graduated with high honors from our program, and had been awarded a scholarship to Emerson College. She had suffered a fatal brain hemorrhage while working nights at a Boston restaurant to earn rent and food money. Most of her former classmates were seated together in the back of the church. One young man had flown in from San Francisco where he had just started a television job. When the minister said very little about their fallen friend, concentrating instead on the resurrection of Jesus Christ theme, they arose from their pews en masse, marched out, and from the church stoop sang three resounding renditions of the Dye-vee Crotchet song. Everyone inside heard the prayer of love.

Truthfully, I never thought the song would have such a positive impact on my students when I first introduced it two years into the program. It isn't part of a finely honed behavioral objective, nor had I planned for the students to sing it every time we met. The idea of singing a song in class blossomed one gloomy March day when I surveyed the forty students before me — who seemed so sad. To lighten their hearts, I sang them the Dye-vee Crotchet song, which I used to sing to my daughter Valerie when she was two. When the students' sadness evaporated, I decided to have them sing it. I wrote the lyrics on the board, phonetically, of course; then had them stand and sing, with me (I'm tone deaf) acting as conductor. Their first try was weak; by the fourth try most of them had overcome their shyness — and were hooked. All succeeding classes have had a similar reaction.

In the past thirteen years I have had time to reflect on why the song has had such a powerful impact on my students. Obviously, it isn't the song *per se* that moves them, for it is a silly ditty. It is the act of singing, in the most unlikely place, a place they often identify with pain and fear of impending failure, that arouses them. I think it has the same effect on them that a religious hymn has on a lover of God. The human soul yearns to express itself, especially under trying circumstances. Singing in class reroutes the students' psychic energy from an inward to an outward flow, enabling them to release much of their tension, and make them more open for the information they're exposed to from their teacher and fellow students. And it makes them less inhibited, more willing to comment in class and ask questions.

Singing the song is also a catalyst in transforming the class into a community. It democratizes the learning environment, drawing together on an equal basis those with strong and weak educational backgrounds; and it helps to break down the racial barriers, which always seem impenetrable the first semester. By the end of the first academic year genuine friendships are forged between Blacks, Hispanics and Whites.

The song meant so much to one class that on graduation day the students gave me a professional baton and a coonskin cap, the kind that Davey Crockett wore. To me the gift was a sign of their gratitude for helping them take their first steps toward gaining freedom from prejudice and a sense of unworthiness that had kept them from aspiring for career heights their potential indicated they could achieve.

While I can't help but acknowledge that the song phenomenon in our program came about accidentally, I did sing the song on that gloomy March day. What prompted me to do it? It had to be more than wanting to lighten the hearts of the students, I thought. I wrestled with the question for some time, gaining some insight from a discussion I had with one of our former students who came by to visit one day. We talked about his experiences in our program, and what they meant to him. He mentioned the song, admitting that at first he was reluctant to sing it, but pointed out that he became an enthusiastic singer by watching me conduct with such intensity. He went on to say, "the fact that my teacher was willing to risk making a fool of himself in order to cheer me up demonstrated to me that he cared for me — and everyone else in the class."

"Cared for me," those were the magical words that provided the answer as to what motivated me to want to lighten the hearts of the students. It was love — nothing else. And I wasn't ashamed of the fact, though trying to explain it in professional circles would most likely set off some snickers, or I would be judged by my peers as a sentimental fool.

Where did that love spring from? Not from a university textbook. It was a spiritual impulse, emanating from the soul, which is a vast reservoir of love. I view the students as human beings sincerely searching for ways to improve their lot; and I want to help them find those ways, and more important, help them discover who they really are — a natural human drive that most of us repress because we don't know how to go about finding out who we really are.

I love my students, and most of them know it. Isn't love a source of attraction? Most of them look forward to being in class, even though our program is demanding. How is my love manifested in the classroom? By a genuinely caring attitude for all the students, which was greatly influenced by a teacher who wasn't certified to teach in a public school. Mehdi Firoozi understood that love is the basis of effective teaching. Without it, even a teacher with the highest academic degrees will fail to bond with his students, causing distrust and a serious communications gap, which, in turn, breeds lack of interest in what the instructor is trying to teach. The absence of love in the classroom is a major factor in the deterioration of American formal education.

CHAPTER
SIX

*Love and Caring
in the Classroom*

I first met Mehdi Firoozi in the summer of 1955, at Green
Acre, a Bahá'í school, in Eliot, Maine. Because he was born in
Iran and educated in Russia, Mehdi had a distinctive accent
when he spoke English; a mix of Persian and Russian flavored
his speech. To me, he sounded like the Mad Russian, a
character on the Eddie Cantor radio show, which was popular
in America in the 1940s and early 1950s.

Physically, Mehdi wasn't attractive. He had large hips,
narrow shoulders and a large head crowned with thick pepper
and salt colored hair. When he looked at you, his head was
always cocked to one side. There was a permanent pimple on
the tip of his large hooked nose; and he had big floppy ears.
But there was one bodily feature that was attractive — his
brown eyes, which were rimmed by long black eyelashes. Now,
I know there's truth to the saying, "eyes are the mirror of the
soul," for when I looked into Mehdi's eyes I saw beauty — and
felt loved. Many others who knew him saw and felt the same
thing when they were in his presence. He was especially
popular with young people; they sensed his genuineness, and
were attracted by his positive and non-judgmental attitude and
all-embracing love. And his selflessness was refreshing — a

quality he always manifested when teaching. He wasn't afraid
to use himself as a prop in order to get a point across.

That became evident to me when I first met him in a class
he taught at Green Acre. The course was called "The Pathway
to Immortality," it was actually a week-long explanation of the
life-after-death process. In the audience was a diverse group of
men and women, including two elderly matrons whose faces
looked like they were chiseled out of the granite of nearby New
Hampshire. One of them was wearing a beige bonnet. When I
looked at them and smiled, their faces remained emotionless,
and stayed that way throughout Mehdi's highly animated
lecture. That is remarkable, I thought.

Mehdi's entrance was unique. As soon as he noticed the
students, he dropped to the floor, completely stretched out, and
began wiggling, saying in his special accent, "I'm an embryo in
mine mother's womb." He embraced himself and added, "I'm
loving it in here; it is so warm and comfortable; and I'm getting
mine food in here."

I was both fascinated and trying to keep from laughing, and
when I glanced at those two elderly matrons and saw that they
had remained expressionless, my urge to laugh heightened. I
bit the walls of my mouth to stay in control.

Mehdi, meanwhile, was crawling. "But now I must go into
the world, and leave all of this comfort," he cried out. "I don't
know what to expect; that scares me, but I must go; I can't
stay." He suddenly raised his head and arms to the ceiling and
exclaimed, "The new world is so beautiful! The light is so
much better than the darkness of the womb. And my mother is
hugging me, loving me, and feeding me." He concluded that
section of the lecture by pantomiming an infant suckling from
his mother's breast. In the remaining forty minutes he went on
to explain that our present life is also a womb world, but a
much larger one, with more complex personal responsibilities,
than that we traversed in our prenatal form.

There was no doubt in my mind that without his
demonstration it would have been difficult to grasp the point
he was making. At the start of the second session Mehdi
bounded into the classroom, whipped off his jacket and flipped

it onto the table, and said, "That is mine body!" then dashed to the window, raised it and, before jumping out, cried out, "This is the soul ascending!"

Mehdi's teaching wasn't confined to the classroom. I'll never forget the time he came to the rescue of three suffering souls in the Green Acre dining hall. Little five-year-old Charlie was having a temper tantrum: he refused to eat his supper (pork chops, corn and mashed potatoes). The boy's mother was beside herself; not only was she embarrassed, but she was unable to feed her two-year-old daughter who was upset because her brother was crying. Of the seventy or so adults in the hall, only Mehdi arose to help the distressed family. He bent over the table, took Charlie's hand and said, "Now Charlie, I know you are sad, but just think of what the pig, that the pork chops came from, did for you so you can grow up strong. It sacrificed its life for you."

Charlie stopped crying, ate all of his supper and went off to play. But the boy wasn't the only one who benefited from Mehdi's spontaneous lesson. Mehdi had inspired many of the adults in the hall to be more giving, more concerned about other people's feelings; and he also helped us better understand the meaning of sacrifice in the cycle of life.

Though I try to maintain a loving atmosphere in the classroom, I'm not always smiling and a fountain of sweet words. I share my feelings with the students. If I'm angry because I had a flat tire on my way to school, I tell them about it; if I'm sad because a publisher has rejected my manuscript, I tell them about it. I even share some of my personal spiritual battles with them. Revealing my feelings strengthens our relationship. Mutual trust is forged. My being open with the students encourages them to be open with me and their classmates, allowing them to release some of their pent up feelings, which have been stifling their learning ability. And it is a great release for me; for trying to repress strong feelings and teach effectively is stressful. I can't pretend that nothing is bothering me when something is, and the students know that, too. Why, some of them even sense some of my subconscious concerns. One morning I was surly, snapping at them, and a young man raised his hand, asking, "Is there anything wrong?"

At first I was taken aback, for I could think of no serious conflicts in my life, and the ride to work had been pleasant. And then it dawned on me — I had slept longer than usual, missing my usual prayers and meditations before breakfast. I shut my eyes for a moment; then thanked the young man for sharing his concern for me, and without any reservations shared with the students why I had been so obnoxious the first ten minutes of class.

Whatever firmness I demonstrate as a teacher is based on a desire to help students mature as thinkers and decent, responsible human beings. In time, most of them realized that. For some the realization comes after considerable pain and anger. My policy on lateness causes both. Certainly, it isn't a case of my gaining pleasure from seeing others squirm. In fact, it pains me to do what I have to do to break students of habits that can make them irresponsible. A letter from a doctor is about the only excuse I accept.

I reveal the policy the first day I meet the new students, emphasizing how it will benefit them, and how I will administrate it — mercilessly. When someone comes to class late they must apologize to the class and me. After he's seated, I stare at him for about a minute. No one stirs. It is as if the rest of the students feel they are in the hot seat. Then I ask the tardy student to explain why it is wrong to be late. And he shares our program's lateness litany: "It is discourteous to my fellow students and my teacher, for it interferes with what's going on in class. And as a student of television communications I must have a great appreciation for time. If a program is scheduled for 8 p.m. it must go on at that time and not a second later." If the student has a memory lapse, I recite it. One time, instead of reciting the litany, an outraged student glared at me and shouted, "Bastard!" and stormed out of class, slamming the door so hard I thought the window pane would crack. The next day, she was back in class, on time. As far as I know every student that remains in our program, and has a tardiness habit, overcomes it by the time he or she graduates.

I'm tough in other situations, but never for the sake of being tough. In fact, I find it emotionally draining, because it means going against my basically calm nature. There's always a reason for my sternness. There are times when a boot to the butt is necessary to get a student started on a project, or back on the academic track.

Kim Commiskey came into my office, declaring that she wanted to drop out of college. She had had it with doing homework and didn't see any purpose in being in school. I was acquainted with her background — and also her rich potential. Kim quit high school when she was fifteen, drifting from one unfulfilling job to another. As far as the future was concerned, she was visionless. Yet I sensed that there was something within her that was driving her to do something meaningful, to become someone who could help others be happier. It was obvious that she lacked career direction, but what she needed even more was an awareness of who she really was and the good she had to offer whatever community she was in.

When I refused to sign her withdrawal papers, she grew angry. I sat back and listened to her harangue and accuse me of not being sympathetic. I fired back, "You're afraid of meeting a challenge head on; you're a quitter; you always have been and will continue to be unless you decide right now to quit quitting."

Kim cried — and left my office, leaving her withdrawal papers with me.

She graduated with high honors, went on to Emerson College on scholarship, and eventually became the local program director of a Boston television station. After several years in TV she went back to school to earn a Masters degree so she could do something more fulfilling — teaching communications in a junior high school, the spot in her educational journey where she had grown disenchanted with education.

There are times when I have to play the role of father figure for students who never knew their father, or whose father abandoned their family at an early age. These students, I have learned, don't know how to deal with authority, yet a part of them yearns for it, because it gives them a sense of belonging, satisfying a deep need to identify with an organization. From such an experience they hope to gain the direction and comradeship that has been missing in their fractured family life.

Arthur never knew his father, spending more than half of his 33 years in correctional institutions. He had been out of jail a year when he signed up for our program. Six-foot-eight and 240 pounds, Arthur was, at first glance, a menacing figure. Endowed with considerable street smarts, he had become an accomplished con artist. Like so many people with his kind of background, it was either master the art of conning or perish in the streets.

Arthur was trying hard to live a conventional life, setting up an apartment with his fiancé. He even had his five-year-old son with him, who had been living with his grandmother in California. Arthur was proud of his son; whenever he had an opportunity to speak about him he would. He was particularly proud of his son's excellent progress in school. At times he would show me the youngster's drawings and lesson papers.

Arthur could think quickly on his feet, excelling in our class discussions. But with a poor educational foundation, his writing skills needed considerable work. He knew it, and desperately wanted to improve his writing. His biggest problem was impatience; he wanted to be an overnight writing wonder.

In my first private meeting with Arthur, I told him that I was aware of his conning ability; and that I knew every time he was trying to con me. When he tried to refute what I had said, I shot back, saying, "Now stop that bullshit!"

"What do you mean?" he demanded, sitting up and trying to look mean.

While I was scared, for I hardly knew the guy, and I was aware of his checkered background, something deep down pushed me to press ahead. "Arthur, I know you're a con artist, because it takes one to know one."

He burst out laughing and pointed at me. "You — I can't believe it."

I went on to tell him about my background, pointing out how poorly I had done in school, that I too couldn't write well; and how I relied on my street smarts to survive.

He was impressed and spoke openly about his childhood, and some of the crimes he had committed, and what got him started breaking the law at age eight.

We made a pact that every time he tried to con me I was going to call him on it; and I told him that at first he was going to deny my claim, because it takes time to overcome a deeply entrenched practice, especially one that has been so useful over the years. In time, he grew less defensive when I caught him conning. As he grew more settled in our program and was accepted and respected by his peers, he grew more genuine and rarely conned. When he did slip, he no longer argued; instead, he responded by smiling and saying, "Thank you, pop."

When I decided to take on my students' personal problems in order to be a more effective teacher, I realized that I had to respond to all of those who were signaling for help. To pick up a student's SOS requires listening with the heart as well as the ear. In other words, paying attention to how a student is speaking as well as what he's saying, and also being alert to signs of emotional discomfort in students who aren't participating actively in class discussion. A grim expression or excessive rubbing of the forehead can be signals. After class I approach those I feel are troubled and ask if I may be of help. While some refuse assistance, others are eager to unburden themselves. I have never been accused of prying or told to "mind my own business."

When I first met Sarah, she needed lots of attention — in class and afterwards. Her hand was up every time I'd ask the class a question. Trying to be fair, I didn't call on her all of the time. After class one day she accused me of ignoring her, and so I invited her into my office for a chat. I pointed out that I was aware every time she waved her arm in class but that I couldn't call on her all of the time because one of my objectives was to get everybody involved in our discussions. Besides, I added, I didn't want to give the impression that I favored one student over others. Sarah seemed to accept my reasoning, but wasn't about to leave. She went on to tell me how happy she was to be in our program; that it was so much better than she thought it would be and how she had had trepidations about going back to school. She had graduated with honors from high school eight years earlier and instead of going to college roamed the country seeking adventure and fortune and finally returned home full of wild memories and penniless. But being in our program, she added, represented a new day for her.

When I stood up to indicate that our meeting was over, she insisted that I check over her homework. Sarah was beginning to irritate me.

"I spent all night doing it," she said.

Reluctantly I took her notebook, pretending to read what she had prepared. I couldn't concentrate because I had an important appointment downtown in fifteen minutes, and I didn't want to be late. When I handed the notebook back to Sarah, I simply said, "fine," and started toward the door.

A week later I noticed that Sarah was sullen. She hadn't raised her hand once in class. In fact, she never once looked at me. I felt guilty: had I hurt her feelings during our meeting? I wondered. After class I invited her to my office. At first she hesitated, making lame excuses, but she came along after I insisted that she come.

At first she was non-communicative, spiritless. I tried to cheer her up by telling her how well she was doing in our program, but she remained numb. When I offered to review her homework, she said, "I'm planning to withdraw from school."

"What!" I exclaimed. "But you're making great headway; you have demonstrated a strong aptitude for television communications. Your chances of making it in the field as a writer or producer are good."

"But I can't hack it," she said, finally showing some emotion.

"Is there anything that I have done that prompted your decision to quit?"

"No."

"Don't you like your classes?"

"I enjoy them."

"Then why abandon something you like?"

She looked away, biting her lip, tears streamed down her cheeks.

I moved closer to her, and did something that could have gotten me into deep trouble with the administration. I took Sarah's hand and held it firmly.

After a few minutes, she said, "You see, I have a manic depressive personality. When I'm manic I'm high, but when I'm depressed I'm overwhelmed with feelings of inadequacy. I lose grip of life and slide into a state of hopelessness; everything seems meaningless, and that includes school."

"Then you realize that by quitting college, you are making a mistake?"

"Yes, I can accept that rationally, but emotionally I can't accept it. I have no desire to do anything. For example, I didn't do the assignment that was due today, and the way I feel now I won't be able to do the assignment that's due next week."

"That's okay," I said. "What's important is that you want to complete our program."

"I do."

"Then we'll work together to get you through."

And we did that — but it wasn't easy. It was a tough test to take. There were times when I seriously thought of giving up. I didn't mind the talks we had every time I noticed that she had slipped into her depressive state. Through our discussions she was shored up emotionally and switched from a negative to a positive focus of life. Seeing that change in her made me feel good.

It was some of the destructive things she did in between our talks that bothered me — things that adversely affected our program. For example, midway through the Spring semester, the first year class, the one that Sarah was a part of, wasn't as responsive, as upbeat as it had been earlier in the year. When they sang the song half-heartedly I knew there was a problem. I even asked the class what was wrong, but I couldn't get a definitive answer. During one of my talks with Sarah, I learned the answer. She had grown angry at me, because she felt that I was shirking my duty as a teacher by dismissing class early twice so I could make a lecture date at a different college; and one day I canceled class in order to make an important speech. She was also miffed that I took longer than a week to return the mid term exams. After explaining to her that I had never dismissed class before, and that the college administration had authorized the speaking engagements, and pointed out the extra duty things I did like speaking to her regularly, I asked her point-blank, "Did you share your grievances with your classmates?"

Sarah turned toward the wall; she couldn't look at me. It was clear that she had whipped up a backbiting campaign that was poisoning my relationship with the class. I was almost at the explosion point. A part of me wanted to throw Sarah out of my office and let her drown in her sorrow. Prayer extinguished the rage within me.

"Do you realize the harm you have done by talking behind my back?" I said.

She closed her eyes and said, "But you admit doing those things?"

"But you didn't know the facts, the circumstances. Why didn't you come to me with your complaints?" I paused and looked her straight in the eye. "Haven't I treated you fairly?"

The question broke down her defenses. After a long silence, she turned to me and said, "Please forgive me, that won't happen again."

And it didn't. The next time I met with Sarah's class I spoke for about 20 minutes about the evils of backbiting and how easy it was for all of us to succumb to the spirit-crippling practice.

Sarah graduated with more than honors. She had broken the cycle of not completing important projects that had plagued her all of her life. She had learned to manage better during a depressive slump, and she had grown to respect other people's views and rights, to be more fair-minded.

Not all of my interventions in students' personal problems produced the desired results. One heart-wrenching experience comes to mind.

Gloria joined our program after a trial period. Her performance in the "Speaking on TV" class was excellent. The fact that I told her so, and had given her an A grade, had little effect on her deepseated fear of not being able to cope with new challenges, especially those to do with school. In my mind, she had all of the tools to do well: she was bright, creative, eager to succeed. Her only drawback was her lack of confidence, and I was certain that that flaw could be corrected. After all, we had succeeded in building up confidence in many other students.

But we failed with Gloria. Not because we didn't try. God knows we tried.

Her first semester was a resounding success — all A's. But it didn't come without much encouragement from me. Every time I would introduce a new TV writing method, she would stare at me teary eyed, on the verge of panicking. After class I would have to reassure her that she was capable of doing it, that she had mastered every other method I had introduced to the class. And every time I would say, "call me if you have trouble figuring it out," she would calm down. I suspect Gloria needed to know that her teacher was as close to her as the telephone. She never called me.

While Gloria was an excellent student, I was making no headway in helping her gain confidence and overcome her instability, her fear, which seemed to be choking the very core of her being. I finally found out the root cause of her fear during one of our discussions in my office.

She was married, had two school age children, taught church Sunday School classes, and worked part-time as a waitress. Her husband, an automobile mechanic, who dropped out of college after two years, wasn't making enough money to pay all of the bills. He resented Gloria going to college, for he felt it was keeping her from working full time. In fact, he was outspoken about his opposition toward her furthering her education; he would often badger her to quit. Her only response was to break out in tears and draw further into her cocoon of self-pity. Several times she attempted suicide. While the husband's attitude toward her educational pursuits wasn't the cause of her fear, it certainly was a reinforcing element.

Gloria's fear stemmed from her father's continual sexual abuse of her between the ages of eight and nineteen.

Two weeks into the second semester, this fragile soul cracked half way through a writing class. I took her to my office. After calming down, she apologized for breaking down and, in tears, said she had to drop out of school. I agreed, despite my belief that everything should be done to keep a student in school. Never before had I bowed so quickly and easily to a student's request to quit our program. But Gloria's case was special. Had I applied any pressure on her to stay, it would have been disastrous for her and the program.

We remained friends. She wrote me from the sanitorium where she was receiving psychiatric help; and when released, she came to visit her former classmates and teacher. Gloria had decided to divorce her husband, see a therapist regularly and, in time, return to school. While I was genuinely happy to see her again, I didn't offer an opinion on the decisions she had made, other than that I was glad that she had made them. To me that was a good sign, because in the past she had had difficulty making decisions.

I gained some important insights from the episode involving Gloria. First, the importance of being flexible in the way we treat our students. What works for one student may not work for another, for everyone's nature isn't exactly alike, nor is his background. Secondly, it was a humbling experience. I was so sure that I would be able to build up her confidence, because of the success I had had with others. Actually, I had grown cocky about my ability to transform troubled students. Lastly, and perhaps the biggest lesson I learned, was that education begins long before a child starts kindergarten. What parents do to prepare their youngsters for formal schooling determines, in large measure, how well they do in school — and in life.

CHAPTER
SEVEN

Teaching Self-Knowledge

Though it's important to provide our students with a solid grounding in the basics of television production, what I view as more important is helping our students start, in earnest, the search for their true selves, and giving them guidance as to how one goes about doing that. Achieving that is the central behavioral objective of our program, and our students know that. I make that clear the first day we meet. At first, most of them can't appreciate our primary objective, because no teacher ever demanded something like that before; and besides, they're primed to learn how to push all the right TV buttons and pull all the right TV levers. They want to get their hands on the studio equipment, and not be bothered with something they deem irrelevant and bordering on the absurd. While their wish to work with the television hardware is fulfilled the first week of classes, they also find themselves engaged in a serious campaign of finding out who they are, a totally unfamiliar process. It's a different kind of learning, which they discover can be both painful and liberating.

Before starting them on their search, I explain why it is important for them, as prospective TV professionals, to become more acquainted with their true selves. Inner strength, stronger self-esteem and confidence, I tell them, are necessary in order to

succeed in television. Without an understanding of who they
are it's extremely difficult for them to manifest these
characteristics. They'll remain timid, afraid to take risks,
resistant to change and will lack the dynamism that's needed to
be successful. So, at first, wishing to succeed becomes the chief
motivation of their becoming involved in the process of
discovering who they really are. After a while they learn to
value the necessity of their search in terms of becoming happier,
more focused human beings.

Accepting this different teaching approach is difficult, at
first. I remember overhearing a student whispering to a
classmate, "It's worse than confession." To the uninitiated, I can
see how that can be, because everyone is revealing personal
aspects of themselves that they have never shared with anyone
else before, not even themselves. But there are good reasons why
we do it that way, and it doesn't take long for the students to
appreciate the method's value.

In every course they take with me during their two years at
STCC, they are involved in something that aids their search.
Witnessing their awareness of their inner growth, as they make
headway in finding out who they really are, brings me great joy.
That kind of experience makes me appreciate how a devoted
gardener must feel when he or she sees the first flower of the
season bloom.

The search has other benefits. Sharing self-knowledge with
each other helps to foster the spirit of family and sense of
community that I try to establish with each class. By hearing
their classmates bare deep feelings, they grow more empathetic,
are able to make progress in overcoming some of their prejudices,
and become more tolerant of their fellow students' idiosyncrasies.
And there are times when students, who are aware of someone's
weaknesses, volunteer to help him or her overcome them. How
we initiate and stimulate the students' search will become
apparent in a forthcoming chapter that describes some of the
courses we teach (see Chapter 9).

Though the majority of students in our program didn't do
well academically in high school, we don't engage them in any
remedial work. On the contrary, they are exposed to high

powered rigor. They have to do a lot of writing; in one class that meets twice a week during the first semester, students must prepare, for homework, two essays of 500 words or more on various profound topics. For another class, during the same week, they have to write a batch of TV scripts. Plus — they have to do some writing for their electives, like English Composition and General Psychology.

There are two reasons for all of that writing: one, to sharpen the students' thinking processes; and second, to improve their writing skills. I'm a firm believer that learning to write is like learning to walk. The more you write the better writer you become. And the stumbling, falling and scrapes are to be expected. We're not born walking out of our mother's womb. Based on experience as a published writer, a seasoned journalist, and someone who couldn't distinguish between a colon and semicolon until his second year in college, I think I know what I'm talking about. As you continue to write, you intuitively sense what the right form is. Results that come from the trial and error approach are easier to internalize for people like me, who view a grammar textbook as an obstruction to creative flow. Oh, you may not be able to identify the nature of each clause and phrase through this approach, but you'll have developed a feeling as to when and how to use them. Most of our students graduate writing better than when they started our program.

The rigor intensifies in the second semester. By the end of their first academic year at STCC, every student has written a textbook on communications; a funding proposal for a 30 second TV public service spot, along with a script of the spot; scores of TV news stories and critiques of TV programs; as well as a 30 minute television drama. On top of all that, they produce and present fifteen extemporaneous talks for the "Speaking on TV" classes, on such weighty topics as the purpose of life. As far as I know there isn't another college program that demands that much production from a first year student. And the great majority of students succeed in achieving those assignments, some doing better than others. But they all do it, providing them with a significant psychological boost.

For many, the accomplishment means a loosening of inferiority's grip on their psyche. It proves to them that they can do what they never felt capable of doing. Their confidence soars. They develop an enthusiasm for learning. Many raise their career expectations. All of them feel better about themselves. Had they been forced to do remedial work they would never have accomplished what they did. I believe that remedial classes in college reinforce feelings of inferiority in some students. It is a form of social segregation. To be placed in a remedial class, they feel, is to be classified as stupid; they sense that the cage door has been shut, that they have been branded backward or dumb for life; and consequently do the kind of work that's expected of students who must take remedial classes.

Now, I'm not opposed to strengthening the educational foundation of students who, for whatever reason, had always done poorly in school. But it should be done off campus, because when they enter college they don't want to be stigmatized, treated as second class students; they are already suffering from low self-esteem. And the kind of approach used by teachers in the preparatory classes is crucial. The teachers must sincerely feel that the students can succeed in college. If they don't feel that way, then the students will sense it, no bonding will take place and the class will become a drudgery for teacher and student. Without hope, the student will have no desire to learn. The hope can be generated by describing as graphically as possible the personal benefits a student derives from succeeding in the preparatory program, as well as by helping the student create a vision of what he hopes to attain professionally. It should be the teacher's responsibility to help the student chart the course that is needed in order to fully implement the vision.

We do that in our program — for all of our students. It is important because it provides them with direction, which helps to alleviate some, if not all, of their anxiety about the future. It also gives them a sense of purpose in life, other than surviving. I have discovered that when a student's anxiety level is down, and he's hopeful, he learns better.

The process is helpful even for those who haven't decided on what aspect of the television field they want to pursue, or for that matter, for those who decide to enter a profession outside of broadcasting. When they make their decision, they simply put the process in motion.

The process is introduced midway through the first semester and is repeated and amplified from time to time during the remainder of the students' stay at STCC. It is essentially developing a goal and a set of objectives, and a deep desire to operationalize them. I use an expanded metaphor to help students clarify and appreciate the value of the process, which also motivates them to become involved in it. I call the process the "crossing of the stream" metaphor.

The goal is crossing a stream that is far too broad to leap across, far too deep to walk across and far too swift to swim across. After a careful survey of the stream, you decide that the safest way to reach the other side is by mentally marking a pathway of stones to it. The stones become the objectives. Now while it is important to keep the goal in mind, what is immediately more important is achieving the next objective. Thus most of your energy, thought and time should be devoted to reaching the next stone. Once you're securely in place, you focus you're attention on the next objective. Making it is going to be a little easier, because you have had experience reaching the first stone and are now a bit closer to the other side — which is reassuring. Every time you reach another stone or achieve another objective you gain more confidence that you'll accomplish your goal, because you are that much closer to it. Many of the doubts that plagued you at the outset have vanished. You are more enthusiastic and hopeful of the future. Once you reach the other side, and reflect on what you have done, you really realize that the objectives were the stepping stones to achieving your goal; you develop a deeper appreciation of each objective and the process in general, which you are now willing to apply in achieving other goals in your life, regardless of their nature.

Our students have found the "crossing of the stream" metaphor helpful in creating their personal career vision. To make sure everyone understands how to apply it to themselves, they must write it out and share it in class so they may gain feedback from their classmates and myself. Then they refine it, and give me a copy so that at the end of the academic year when I have a personal meeting with each student I can check to see if they are on target in achieving their goal. If they are not, I usually suggest that they institute a new objective or two. For most of them, it will have been the first time they have ever pondered their future in such a focused fashion.

Of course before they put their vision on paper, I explain how the "crossing of the stream" metaphor can be applied to their becoming a TV director, producer, videotape editor or a TV news reporter. I give them sample objectives that would fit the pursuit of several television specialties. But I purposely avoid giving them a completed set of objectives, for fear they would copy it, make some cosmetic changes and hand it in as theirs. By doing that they would miss the mind enriching experience of thinking through the process. Without that experience they would have difficulty owning it, and most likely give up pursuing the objectives and never achieve their goals.

To give you some idea of what a career vision blueprint looks like, here is one student's effort. Her goal was to become a TV news reporter.

First Semester Objectives:
1. Do well in my academic studies.
2. Three times a week identify aloud what I see, hear, and feel. It can be done at work, at the playground, while driving. Strive for accuracy.
3. Twice a week cover an event in my life (someone's wedding, funeral, a party, a baseball game) as a news story — writing it down.
4. Work doubly hard in my TV writing class.

During Four Week Break Between Semesters:
1. Read a book on TV news reporting. List questions that the book fails to address and present them to my teacher or a working TV news reporter.

Second Semester Objectives:

1. Continue the rewriting exercises done in the TV writing class, at least three times a week.

2. Become a reporter on the college newspaper.

3. Watch a network newscast six times a week not as a regular viewer but as an analyst, employing the format we use in our analysis class.

Twelve Week Summer Break:

1. Do an internship at a local TV newsroom.

2. Arrange to write copy for a newscast and track down sources for news stories.

3. Interview at least three reporters attached to the newsroom to find out how they broke into the business and ask their opinion of what's the best way to prepare myself to become a TV reporter. Do the same with the News Director.

4. Make a survey of journalism schools. Select five to apply to.

Third Semester Objectives:

1. Continue the internship at the TV newsroom (earning three credits).

2. Work doubly hard in the TV Journalism course, getting the highest grade possible.

3. Critique local TV newscasts three times a week, employing the analysis class format. Stress how the newscasts can be improved, especially the reporters' feeds.

4. Arrange to use our department's remote equipment to practice the capture-of-news-on-video exercise learned in the TV Journalism class. This should be done at least twice.

During Four Week Break Between Semesters:

1. Read another book on TV news reporting.

2. All Journalism school applications completed and mailed.

Fourth Semester Objectives:

1. Do the best job possible as a reporter on the college TV newscast.

2. Put together a portfolio of the best work done on the

newscast and newspaper.

3. Visit Journalism schools. Interview professors and students before making a decision.

Summer Break Objectives:

1. Try for a summer replacement job in a TV newsroom — dispatcher, production assistant. First check the place where I had interned. If I can't get a job, resume the internship and try to arrange on my own time accompanying a reporter covering a series of stories. Try to do this at least six times during the summer.

2. Pick up letters of reference from News Director and other key personnel at TV station.

Journalism School Objectives:

1. Take electives that will describe how governments and societies function.

2. Become a reporter on the journalism school's newspaper for one year; and in my last year become a reporter on the school's campus-wide newscast.

3. Prepare a portfolio of the best work I did for the newscast and newspaper. Weave in good stuff done at STCC.

4. During the last semester prepare resumé and begin making job inquiries among small market TV stations.

After Receiving My Bachelor's Degree:

1. Get a job in a small market where I can shoot camera, edit video as well report and write.

2. Spend about eighteen months at small market station before jumping to a medium market station.

The student who prepared this set of objectives is now working in a large television market. With a carefully crafted career vision blueprint, a student has a perspective of an important aspect of her future. It functions as a map does to a driver on a long journey.

CHAPTER
EIGHT

Learning through Cooperation and Consultation

Aside from singing a song, my classroom approach is, putting it mildly, different. I doubt if it is listed in the textbooks used in university education methods classes. A respected and gracious educationalist would probably classify it as "unorthodox."

Through 21 years of front line experimentation, I have developed an approach that helps students to think more deeply, critically and creatively. It is purposely done without textbooks. While in the communications field they seem useful for cramming for exams, based on my experience, they inhibit deep and creative thought. I have never used a textbook in any of my classes. This doesn't mean that I have a prejudice toward books. On the contrary — I recommend that my students expose themselves to great thinkers' thoughts through reading. For every book report a student does, he or she earns extra credit. The kinds of books I recommend stimulate deep thinking, guide the mind into realms most readers have never explored before, and trigger creative flow. In some students, who once had an aversion toward reading, their experience with books like *The Seven Mysteries of Life*, *A Guide for the Perplexed*, *The Turning Point*, or *The Global Brain* have generated a desire to read more.

Instead of using a textbook, I have my first semester students write one on communications. This is done, because I believe — and again, this is based on personal experience — that when you research, ponder and write about something, you stand a better chance of retaining it; for what you've done is based on discovery, which sets off excitement and enthusiasm; and what we become enthusiastic about usually becomes a part of us — we end up owning it. And what we own, we try to save.

About a month into the first semester I announce to the students that they are in the process of writing a textbook. To lessen the shock, I mention, just prior to the announcement, that they are involved in a project that will seem impossible for them to complete. But when I explain that students in previous classes, who had the same negative reaction to the textbook project idea, ended up doing it, a glimmer of hope registers in their eyes. They feel challenged, especially those who have a poor self-image and desperately want to feel equal with others. Their interest in the project seems to perk up after I describe what they will derive from the exercise — more confidence, for one thing. They will accomplish something that, at one time, they felt incapable of doing. And through their accomplishment they will experience the kind of rush that an inexperienced climber gets when he reaches the peak of a mighty mountain. Their research and writing skills will improve. They will internalize the kind of knowledge that is essential to both their career and their development as a human being. Because they all want that, they gain a little more assurance. Filling them in on my role in the project also helps to lessen their apprehension. Finally, I implore the students to have faith in what I'm asking them to do, reminding them that I am on their side, that I care about them, that I want them to succeed, that I want them to grow as much as their potential will allow them to grow. After that, they seem more trusting of me, and feel a little more comfortable about the project.

Now, I'm aware that my appeal to them isn't going to completely eradicate their skepticism and fear. The pep talk is designed to penetrate their feelings of inadequacy and apprehension and move them to try to do something new. For the most part, the talk does what it's supposed to do. Students make a beginning and, in time, after many battles with persistent doubts, they become more courageous; and when they are nearing the end of the writing effort, many of them become euphoric, for they recognize that they are about to complete the impossible. In fact, some of them — after completing their book — have asked me for addresses of publishing houses. In monitoring this annual project, I have learned that it boosts a student's low self-esteem, builds up their confidence and makes them less fearful of taking on future demanding academic challenges. I make sure to tell them that this kind of conditioning will be useful in the work place. Employees who aren't afraid of tackling new problems and challenges are in a better position to gain leadership roles. To back up the pronouncement, I cite examples from my work experiences.

It's important to note that my pep talks are impromptu efforts to bolster students' confidence, to motivate them to carry on with their tasks, to prepare them emotionally to take on complicated new challenges; not to turn myself into an academic deity with a faithful flock of followers. What I do springs from a sincere desire to serve students. Again, a matter of love. Not the Romeo and Juliet variety; it is the kind that Mehdi Firoozi expressed, and which years later, Dr. Scott Peck wrote about in his book, *The Road Less Travelled*. He defined love as helping oneself and others to grow spiritually. It's not a case of exposing students to a particular religious dogma. It has to do with helping them discover their spiritual nature and providing guidance as to how to develop it. I believe without that knowledge a human being functions much like an animal. Later on in the book this matter is dealt with in depth (see Chapter 10).

I don't pretend to know everything; and my students know that, because the first time we meet I share my educational philosophy with them. I point out that we are part of a learning partnership, that we learn from each other. It isn't always an equal partnership, I add, because my having more education than them, more work experience than them, means they will probably learn more from me than I will learn from them. It doesn't take long for them to accept the notion that they're involved in a learning partnership, because there are legitimate knowledge exchanges between us. Whenever I learn something from a student I thank her in class. I never try to cover up a mistake; I openly acknowledge it and apologize to the students. That kind of candor strengthens the trust between us.

Our class meetings are organized to accommodate our partnership. Students are conditioned to listen whole-heartedly to what their classmates have to say in class. They listen to each other with practically as much intensity as they listen to me. They take notes of everyone's contribution — but they don't start off with that kind of mind-set. There are habits to break. The biggest one is letting up on their concentration when the teacher stops talking, and not paying attention to what their fellow students are saying. Another bad habit has to do with their attitude toward reading essays in class. They are so fearful of being called on next that it's impossible for them to concentrate on what's being read, at times missing valuable knowledge. For the first two months of the first semester I acknowledge their feelings of fear and apprehension before calling on students to read their homework — and encourage them to listen to each other with an open mind, free of fear, and looking forward to learning something from other students' readings.

Of course, I'm aware that getting rid of a deepseated fear requires more than someone telling you to get rid of it. As far as most of my students are concerned, their timidity is based on a low grade fear that can be overcome by continual heartfelt appeals by someone they trust. Before commenting on each essay, I preface my remarks by reminding them that I'm not trying to humiliate the reader or hurt him in any way. We are all learning together, I say. By allowing yourselves to be critiqued in the classroom, I add, you are committing an act of sacrifice. The questions I ask, the comments and corrections I make, I point out, could help others avoid making the same mistakes. After each critique, I thank the reader for helping us grow more knowledgeable. And that statement isn't made in a facetious manner, nor is it viewed as such by the students. At first the statement elicits some nervous laughter. But by the second semester the giggling no longer follows the remark.

In our program more stress is placed on cooperation than competition. Whatever competition exists rests with oneself, and is practiced in implementing a student's career vision blueprint, and in strengthening one's character weaknesses, something all our students become acquainted with in their first semester. Other than these personal exercises, they try to cooperate with each other, even when taking exams and writing papers. It isn't easy to shed the individualistic attitude that was drummed into us since kindergarten or earlier. Our students come to our program thinking that winning, being number one in something, is what matters most in their community; and most of them have no qualms about cheating or breaking rules in order to win, as long as they don't get caught. Compounding the challenge of changing their attitude is the influence of television programs, magazines and movies that glorify the "me first" and "winning at all cost" attitudes; and the behavior of their friends, neighbors, and in most instances, their parents, doesn't help, because they have become a part of the prevailing selfishness and desire for continuous personal gratification syndrome.

It's a struggle to get our students to cooperate with each other in their quest for an Associate's Degree but, in time, we're able to get them to try to change their attitude. When they experience the advantages that cooperation presents over competing with one another they begin to internalize the new way. For most, conversion takes place after two semesters.

Before launching the cooperative learning method, I explain how it will benefit them in college, in the work place, and in their community; pointing out that American business corporations are abandoning the "Rugged Individualism" approach, for the highly successful Japanese economic style, which places heavy emphasis on employee cooperation. I introduce them to group consultation as a means of arriving at decisions, and point out how that interpersonal communications skill can bolster a cooperative effort and strengthen the unity of their class, family and community. Through the consultative process everyone's contribution is sought and appreciated.

I also draw upon personal professional experiences in television journalism to illustrate how cooperation can make the difference between producing outstanding and mediocre news coverage. Because they all want to succeed, they become more inclined to cooperate. How do our students practice cooperation? Their critiquing of one another's work is done in the spirit of service; they want to help, not hurt, their fellow students. They study in groups of four or five, in homes or coffee shops, sharing their knowledge with each other. A lot of learning goes on in these sessions, because consultation stimulates discourse. They learn from each other, becoming, in a sense, unofficial teachers. Even the most timid offers ideas. The interchanges within the group trigger far more deep thinking than in class. The reasons for that, I feel, are that to many students the teacher is an intimidating figure, regardless of how benign he seems, and there's more time available outside of a classroom to ponder a question.

The same groups take exams together. Instead of being horrific affairs, tests turn into big learning experiences. As they ponder the questions together, ideas are shared, knowledge is exchanged, answers are arrived at through consultation. After the exams, our students tend to be more enlightened and less drained. In doing papers, they critique each other's work. If someone is stumped, he'll call his classmates for help, and think nothing of it. My hope is that he tries to reach whoever he feels is the brightest one in his group. If he masters that ability, then he will have learned how to gain information from reliable sources, a valuable skill in the work world. What they're doing is not cheating, I point out. In the "work world," especially in television, the teamwork approach is employed. For example, a team of writers is used to create programs. They brainstorm to come up with acceptable story lines. Each one writes a script. After critiquing what they wrote, they may decide to take elements from each effort and put them together as a finished script; or they may select one writer's effort and go with it, making only minor changes.

My placing greater emphasis on learning rather than grades is a major factor in our students' willingness to scrap the competitive attitude for the cooperative process. Now this doesn't mean that I don't evaluate our students. I do — but in a non-traditional way. Because it is highly subjective at times, I could get in trouble with the college's administration if a disgruntled student complains to my superiors. In 1983, a student almost "blew the whistle." Iris was a strong A student. She was mature, in her mid-thirties, had done well in high school and wasn't afraid to speak her mind. And she also had a highly cultivated sense of justice. When she learned that a student in our program, who, she felt, was far less qualified than her, received an A from me she made plans to complain to the head of our division. Fortunately, one of her friends tipped me off. A couple of hours before her meeting with my boss, I spoke to her for almost an hour, sharing with her my grading philosophy. Before leaving my office, Iris called the Division Chairman and canceled her appointment with him.

Despite her action, I was still troubled; actually, conscience-stricken. Running an underground student evaluation system, I felt, was deceitful. I decided to discuss my grading philosophy with the Division Chairman, who had always been reasonable in our dealings, and extremely generous in giving our department what it needed in terms of equipment and supplies. Nevertheless, I was apprehensive about our meeting, for he had the reputation of being a literalist when it came to following the college's policies and procedures. What I had going for me was my department's solid performance over a nine-year period. I knew that he was proud of our program — at least, that's what other teachers told me. When we met, I was too nervous to engage in the customary "small talk" that precedes the major topic of a one-on-one meeting. I got right to the point, acknowledging that I knew that what I was doing was stretching the college's evaluation policy beyond its limits. On the other hand, I didn't forget to reveal how my grading method had helped to transform some of my students' lives.

When I finished explaining my approach, he was looking out the window. The thought of being fired flashed through my mind.

Still peering out the window, he said, "So you know you're doing something wrong."

"I do," I said.

"But what you're doing is helping your students."

"That's right."

After a long pause, he said, "Well, isn't that the main reason for teaching?"

I wanted to shake his hand, but before I could say or do anything, he looked me straight in the eye and said with deep conviction: "Now, if the big wigs in the administration building hear about what you're doing, I'll swear on a stack of Bibles that this conversation never took place."

It wasn't what I wanted to hear, for though I left his office relieved that he was accepting of what I was doing, I still had to conceal my grading approach from the college's higher echelon, which wasn't the healing balm I was seeking for my aching conscience. In time I repressed the matter, continuing to grade as usual. Fortunately for everyone, the head of our Division never had to "swear on a stack of Bibles."

Much of my evaluation system is based on a student's intellectual and emotional growth, and the effort he or she puts forth to grow. Of course, to carry out this approach fairly, you need an understanding of the student's knowledge base and state of mind. That's ascertained from personal talks with students, their early performance in class, especially the essays they read about themselves; and I also rely on intuition. The more growth they make, the higher grade they get.

Effort, they learn — from my appeals in class — is needed in order to grow. Continual effort. Musicians, athletes and writers, I point out, succeed because they have the will to succeed and the willingness to practice every day to perfect their performance. Some wise person once said that "genius is one percent inspiration and 99 percent perspiration." You can't continue to be successful if you discontinue practicing your craft on a regular basis. Though in his seventies, trumpet genius John Burkes (Dizzy) Gillespie, practices every day.

I use examples like that in class to inspire students to make a commitment to continually try harder to grow intellectually

and emotionally, and master their craft. By the end of the first
semester they have an understanding of a basic law of life, that
they know must be applied to themselves if they are to
succeed, namely, "there are two optior in life — progression
and retrogression." What seems to be dormant, isn't. It's really
in a state of decline. A muscle that isn't used atrophies. A
human being is meant to be dynamic, continually growing
wiser by gaining understanding of new aspects of reality. By
the end of the first academic year, most students are more
concerned with trying harder than attaining high grades. This
is an important accomplishment, I tell them, because their
new attitude will be far more useful to them after graduation
than high grades, especially if they apply it to whatever they
do. Of course, there's no danger of their getting poor grades if
they continually try harder to internalize and practice
effectively the knowledge they are exposed to. On the
contrary, their grades will soar.

The risky aspect of my grading scheme has to do with
giving a student who is technically doing C work an A,
because I feel he has the potential to do much better but lacks
the confidence to do it. His being categorized as a poor
learner by previous teachers is a barrier to his doing better
work, because it sets up a vicious circle: he believes their
evaluation of him. An A, I feel, could make him a believer in
himself. Invariably, every time I give a student with a weak
educational background an A, he begins to shine in class and,
in time, does real A work.

Had I not followed my intuition, I know that scores of men
and women, who are successful today, would be "leading lives
of quiet desperation." As you can surmise, I no longer keep
secret my "unorthodox" grading system. What helps me to
speak openly about it is an event that took place about ten
years ago at the University of Massachusetts. The Bahá'ís of
Amherst were holding a memorial service for Robert Hayden,
the great American poet, who was a Bahá'í, and friend to a
number of men and women in the community. We asked
Julius Lester, a professor and noted author, and former student
of Mr. Hayden at Fisk University, to be the chief speaker. In

his talk, Mr. Lester reminisced about his relationship with Mr.
Hayden, stressing the powerful impact the poet had had on his
own life.

He taught me a lifelong lesson in a note attached to a
paper I turned in to him during my senior year.
Whatever the paper was about, I know that I did the
least possible to fulfill the assignment. It was my last
year, and whether I graduated or not, I was leaving. That
was all I knew and all I cared about. My work reflected
this attitude. Mr. Hayden wrote:

"Julius
"I am upset by this 'performance,' because you are
obviously the ablest and most original thinker in this class,
not excluding the poor old broken-down instructor. Yet
you seem to be throwing everything you have away — or at
least not using all your resources. Even this paper has
gleams and flashes of wit and insight which do not appear
on anyone else's. If I thought that giving you a D would
make you perk up, believe me, I'd slap one on you. But I
know it wouldn't accomplish anything for you in your
present state of mind. Whatever you may think of
Victorian lit. as such, you must not commit the
unpardonable (to me) 'sin' of not using all your superb gifts
at all times. What is not used atrophies, as you well know.

"Besides all this, I need your support in this and
other classes you have with me. When you of all people
don't do your work you add to my feelings of frustration.
Can you understand what I mean by this?"

I don't think I had ever experienced such shame as
during the moments I read those words. And it was in
those moments that I ceased to be an adolescent and
began to take myself seriously as an adult.

It is the rarest of teachers who so gives of himself to a
student that he can say: "I need you." And, of course, I
responded.

He gave to me in a different way at the end of that year. To graduate I had to pass comprehensive exams in English and American literature; the latter was supervised by Mr. Hayden. I remember walking into the examination room and looking at the exam. There was not one question on it I could even understand. A brief consultation with myself made it obvious that there was only one thing to do: write my name very neatly on the cover of the Blue Book, hand it to Mr. Hayden who sat at the head of the long oak table, and go walk in the sun.

Late that day I happened to see him. "Well, young man, you really did it this time," he said gaily. I could find no words.

"I gave you a C," he said finally. "If I flunked you and made you stay another year, you'd flunk next year, wouldn't you?"

. . . Thus I graduated, not because I had earned my degree but because Mr. Hayden thought I was more than the sum of my academic performance. Thus he taught me how to express caring . . .

CHAPTER
NINE

The Teacher as
Cheerleader and Coach

By describing in some detail a few of the subjects I teach, I can give a better idea of my classroom attitude and behavior and educational philosophy. "Communicating in Today's World" is the foundation course of our academic program. Though it is listed as an overview of all major elements of communications, it is the course where students begin their search for their true selves, and are introduced to the process of weaving a career vision.

Initially, we grapple with understanding what a human being is. Since most of the students have never seriously thought about the subject, they are woefully unprepared to become professional communicators. How can you effectively communicate to a human being, I point out, if you don't really know what a human being is? Sadly, I add, their ignorance of human nature is shared by many men and women working today in sensitive policy-shaping and program- development posts in local and national television. What is also lacking is an understanding of the nature of the medium in which they work, not to mention how the two natures mesh — and how TV impacts on the viewer. I state in class that one of our objectives is to graduate men and women who will enter the television field more enlightened, more communications sensitive than the present-day professionals, and prepared to tactfully share with their co-workers what they know. In a sense, I point out, we're producing TV communications pioneers.

Our students' first assignment from me is to define and describe what a human being is in 500 words or more. They are discouraged from using a dictionary or an encyclopedia, for I want them to experience the emotions that are aroused from deep thought, and the thrill that comes from generating a good idea or gaining an important insight. I want them to dig into their memory bank, add to it, and rely on it more. What they write is shared in class. The fact that what they share isn't evaluated in terms of right and wrong makes it easier for them to read their essays. It's hoped that through the interchange of ideas everyone's knowledge of a human being will grow.

After I share my view of what a human being is, which is a 30 minute talk, I suggest several books to read on the subject, and encourage them to make their own choice of readings. Then they discuss their findings and ideas in groups outside of class, and rework their essay based on the information they have been exposed to. They're encouraged to continue collecting data and refining the essay until the last day of classes. By the end of the semester, most students have a better understanding of what a human being is, which not only moves them to find out who they are but what exactly to look for in their search.

The process employed in learning the first topic of the course is applied to all of the other topics. Instead of me introducing it via a lecture, with students furiously taking notes and parroting only my views in an essay, they come to grips with what they know of the subject, which often stimulates a desire to know more. While their initial effort may be shallow, they at least make a start, which functions as a framework for the information they gain from other sources. In a sense, learning becomes a sculpting experience. What they end up with is a lot more intelligible and defined than what they start with.

Some of the other topics covered are: Who Am I?; What is Communications?; What's the Difference Between Communications and Expression?; Non-Verbal Interpersonal

Communications; Developing a Demographic Profile; The Nature of Television; How does TV Impact on Humans?; The TV Commercial; An Exploration of Commercial and Public Television; Instructional TV; Use of the Communications Satellite in TV; Grassroots TV through Cable Television.

After they have written their fifth essay, I inform our students that they are writing a book; and that what they have already written, and will continue polishing until the end of the semester, constitutes about a third of the completed text; and that every essay produced henceforth will make up the remaining chapters. To complete the textbook, they have to produce a title, a table of contents, a bibliography and references, and label each chapter. At the end of the semester, it is handed to me typed, constituting their final exam.

Through the "Communicating in Today's World" course, our students begin to appreciate the value of research, not by doing "research papers," but through producing projects that are relevant to the real world — like writing a book or drafting a demographic profile for a proposed show. Trying to produce a TV program without accurate demographics of your target audience, I tell them, is like trying to hit the bullseye with a dart while blindfolded. Since most of the students want to produce appealing programs, they take the demographics exercise seriously. Before drawing up a profile of their home town, they listen to me speak on how a culture is formed. It is one of the few times when I lecture on a topic before the students do a homework assignment on it. In order to shape a workable profile, I point out, you need to discover your target audience's cultural characteristics and understand how they were fashioned through the influence of the local topography, climate, religion, politics, education, industry, transportation and media. They are told that their end product must reflect all of those influences in order to be effective. Then I give them a few tips of possible sources, i.e. city hall, the chamber of commerce, the library.

Outwardly, "Speaking on TV" appears to be another speech course. It's much more than that. It has a number of meaningful objectives. Namely, reinforcing a lot of what was learned in "Communicating in Today's World"; students finding out more about themselves and their classmates; sharpening their improvisational thinking ability; building confidence; learning how to communicate in a clear and cogent fashion; constructing a plan on how to overcome one's character weaknesses; strengthening their persuasion skills. Everyone has several turns putting into practice what they have learned in their Video Techniques course, by working camera, VTR, audio and the switcher when they are not standing before a microphone.

It's not easy to stand in front of a cold, gray camera, speak without notes and explain in two minutes what a human being is, or the meaning of life. Memorizing is discouraged, because we want our students to learn to think sharply — on the spot. Preparation for the weekly presentation is done outside of class, some of it with several classmates, each one providing helpful feedback. To properly prepare, a student is urged to first think deeply about the topic, make a logical outline, then draw it into his consciousness and practice speaking, keeping in mind the importance of hitting the two minute time limit on the nose. Students are evaluated on effort, content, continuity, poise, presentation and timing. I critique everyone, in front of the class, reinforcing the positive aspects and pointing out where improvement is needed and how that can be achieved. The critiquing is purposely done in class so that all can benefit from each other's mistakes.

Invariably, the first three or four presentations are the toughest. But by the end of the semester most students pass, making considerable progress. Again, surmounting an obstacle that at the beginning of the semester seemed insurmountable — another confidence booster. But victory usually comes after a struggle — for some, an agonizing struggle.

Yvonne was a dreamer with lots of ambition, but her lack of confidence prevented her from realizing her dreams. She dreamed of being a talk show host; Oprah Winfrey was her hero. But Yvonne showed no signs of assertiveness; in fact she was reticent to speak up, even when called on. My telling her that she had an opportunity to demonstrate her ability to fulfill her dream in the "Speaking on TV" course didn't break through the shell of shyness she had built around herself. When her turn came to present for the first time, it was sheer torture, not only for her, but for everyone watching, including me. She knew the rules: you sit before the camera for two minutes, regardless of whether you have anything to say or not. In her first try Yvonne couldn't utter a word. She froze, staring helplessly at the camera. Some student behind me — I was sitting at the controls — whispered, "The son-of-a-bitch!" It was obviously a reference to me and my apparent hard-heartedness. I pretended that I hadn't heard the student's expression of compassion, and kept pulling for Yvonne to say something. But she didn't.

The same thing happened the following week. She wasn't a quitter, because she was back the third week. In a way, I was hoping she would skip class, because I didn't want to put everyone through the same torture again. After 30 seconds of silence, Yvonne spoke for about fifteen seconds, paused for a second or two and continued speaking until her time was up. When she entered the control room, everyone applauded; some of the students embraced her. Yvonne broke through her shell and never slipped back. A year later she was doing regular stand-up reports on the college newscast. Shortly before she graduated, Yvonne thanked me for keeping her on what she called the "hot seat." She added: "You always had faith in me."

What she didn't know was that I had almost given up on her. Yvonne taught me an important lesson: stick with the student who isn't making much headway as long as she's sincerely trying hard to succeed. In time there'll be some kind of breakthrough. Though Yvonne may never become another Oprah Winfrey, she graduated with a lot more confidence, and better prepared to attain a respectable portion of her career goal.

The "Speaking on TV" course tests most students' survival instincts. During the first few weeks the tension becomes so intense that many students begin thinking about dropping out of our program. To prevent those thoughts and feelings from pushing them over the edge, I acknowledge their feelings of insecurity by explaining that it is natural to feel like quitting, that their predecessors felt the same way, and that because they persevered, they gained a great deal. Then I point out what they had gained and that they too can experience the same kind of growth. My appeal seems to put most students back on track, but not without some apprehension. Of course, I'm aware that there will always be a few who can't make it, and no amount of pleading on my part will prevent them from quitting.

Sean was a case in point. In his mid-thirties, he was a lover of philosophical books. Before emigrating to America, he spent a year at an Irish university. After several years of working odd jobs, he decided to try for a TV career, and matriculated to STCC. With a powerful intellect and sharp wit, he seemed like he had a promising future in broadcasting television. Some of his essays done for the "Communicating in Today's World" course were brilliant. And when he had something to say in class, all of us listened intently, often learning something meaningful. Taking the "Speaking on TV" course seemed to be his downfall.

Of all the courses he would have to take in our program, I thought, "Speaking on TV" would give him the least trouble, because he was articulate and loved to talk. I'll never forget his first presentation. After his ten second introduction, we seemed to lose sound. I turned to the student who was riding audio, and he assured me that there were no technical problems. Meanwhile, I checked the monitor, and Sean seemed to be talking, with some degree of passion. When he finished, the studio crew burst into uproarious laughter. It turned out that Sean had lost his train of thought, couldn't recall what he wanted to say and pretended to be speaking by moving his lips and gesticulating. No one had ever done that before — or since. After that experience, he never showed up at the "Speaking on TV" class, and appeared only sporadically in the other classes I taught. He didn't return the following semester. About a year later his brother told me that Sean had married, and was tending bar somewhere in New Hampshire.

Most of the topics a student speaks on are designed to help him learn more about himself and strengthen his character, topics like — describe who you think you are; share with us who your favorite hero is and identify those character attributes that make him so appealing; describe three of your character strengths, and explain how they are manifested; describe three of your character weaknesses, and explain how they are manifested; explain what you plan to do to overcome those weaknesses. I take note of each one's plan, and, from time to time, check with each student to see if he's holding fast to his promise. My checking is a gentle nudge, a conscience prick, certainly no harangue. In a sense, when a student reveals his plan, he's forging a covenant with his class. There have been cases when students have volunteered to help classmates follow their character improvement charter.

Some topics are designed to help students develop self-control as well as their creative potential. For example, in two minutes they must try to persuade viewers to purchase "chicken-fat-saturated pickles," without resorting to humor. But there are light moments. One of the topics calls for relating the funniest experience in their lives. The last topic, which is the final exam, is designed to strengthen the spirit of family in the class. The students must do a character profile of a classmate. To do the four minute presentation, they have to interview their subject's parents, friends, brothers and sisters, if there are any. Pictures and other props can be used. I'm not the only one who critiques a student's performance. Each student has an opportunity to critique himself. All presentations are video-taped and available in a special room with a monitor and a playback unit. Students are urged to review their talks. From this procedure, a student not only sees where he's faltered and makes proper adjustments, but over a four-month period he can gauge his rate of growth. I can't think of a single student who has completed this course, who hasn't made some headway as a speaker on TV. When students see the difference between their first effort and last one, their confidence level rises.

If I were more courageous I'd join my students as a regular presenter. The few times I have done it, I have drawn applause of appreciation. I think they like that kind of teacher involvement because it strengthens the bond of trust between us. But doing it regularly would benefit them in a different way: they would be exposed to a fairly decent model of what they are expected to do every week in their "Speaking on TV" course. Maybe one of these years, I'll generate enough courage to implement what my gut tells me is the right thing to do. In the past I have had similar inner conflicts, which I resolved with a leap of faith. For three years I struggled over instituting cooperative exams. The only thing I regret is that I didn't take the leap sooner. Over the years lots of students have missed out on a valuable mind-expanding and social enrichment experience.

All students take two TV writing courses their first year. In the Fall, an introductory course; in the Spring, a more advanced course. Much of what they learn is used the following year when they produce the campus TV newscast. Why must everyone take writing courses, even the most technically oriented student who hasn't the slightest interest in writing — and abhors the very idea of having to put a single word on paper? Because what they are exposed to sharpens their thinking processes and helps them to express themselves clearly. Even a TV engineer, I point out, will find himself in a situation when he must accurately report via memo the extent of a particular technical problem. A poorly written memo could lead to costly mistakes.

In the introductory course, no TV script writing is done for the first three weeks. That time is devoted to the non-mechanical aspects of writing — in other words, how to condition yourself to write. Before anything else, I share with the class how inept I was in English Composition while in school, that it was my worst subject, and despite those earlier handicaps I became a writer. That revelation is the source of encouragement to quite a few students. What is even more comforting is my description of how I felt when I had to write something in high school. Because they can identify with what I had to endure, they are drawn closer to me and become more trusting of me.

To get yourself in the proper frame of mind to write, I point out, you need to have an awareness of your strengths and weaknesses, your likes and dislikes. In other words, you need to have some idea of who you really are. With that self-knowledge you're able to develop an effective rhythm for writing. There is no ideal rhythm that you can adopt and expect to work for you. Not even Shakespeare's. Since no two people are exactly alike, every writer requires a different rhythm, much like a baseball pitcher. He has his own distinctive rhythm to get in the "groove," to get what has to be done effectively. Usually, when his rhythm is upset, he fails to carry out his mission. Sharing my rhythm with our students helps them arrange theirs in terms of how one goes about structuring it.

For example, I write early in the morning, because that's when I'm most energetic and creative. For me, writing in the evening produces far more frustration than polished prose. Because I'm easily distracted by external influences, my writing place is in the basement, far from the noisy kitchen and living room; it's equipped only with materials needed for writing. My children call my office "the black pit," and they stay clear of it, which doesn't disappoint me. When I enter, I have sort of a Pavlovian reflex experience — a desire to write comes over me (it's good for nothing else.)

But before I write a word on the computer, I sharpen two pencils and feel their points with my right forefinger. It doesn't matter that I never use them, it's part of my rhythm. Now this procedure is not a superstition — a practice that's designed to bring about good fortune. It's a technique that aids in my becoming focused. While I have no scientific explanation for why it works, all I know is that it does what it's supposed to do.

One of the students' first assignments is to organize their rhythm for writing, write it down, and be prepared to share it with everyone else. Listening to his classmates' writing rhythms fortifies a student's resolve to integrate it into his life. From time to time, I'll ask individual students in class how their rhythm is working — and if they have made any changes. Their responses usually inspire their fellow students to make needed adjustments. Another early assignment is to write an essay on what they like and dislike about writing. For most, this exercise acquaints them with their true feelings about writing. Often they realize that it's not the act of writing they don't like but, rather, the response to their effort by teachers and others. A reminder of my school days experience with writing, and our program's cooperative approach, usually helps them overcome their reluctance to write. Unshackled from doubts and fear, some students bloom as writers.

They not only learn the fundamentals of TV news and documentary writing, they also apply what they learn to real life projects. In their first year of college, they're exposed to the professional realities of television production. Before writing, for example, a 30-second public service spot, I impress upon them the importance of getting what they produce aired by a local TV station or cable system. (This is one of our ways of taking education out of the realm of abstraction.) Though at first most students feel incapable of achieving such a goal, they gain more confidence when they become acquainted with the practical steps that must be taken to acquire the funding to produce a spot. They learn how to write a proposal, which not only functions as a sales tool but also as a blueprint for the development of the product.

Having written a number of proposals, I share with them how one creates the right kind of impression through the proposal. It must reflect a solid knowledge of the proposed spot's theme, the technical and creative ability to produce an effective product and a basic honesty and genuine desire to do the spot. They are given two weeks to produce a convincing and comprehensive rationale, which entails a considerable amount of research; a week to put together a goal and set of objectives, as well as a treatment. The following week they have to come up with a biographical sketch of those involved in producing the spot — plus a budget. Then they write the spot, using as a guide the treatment, which reflects the proposal's goal and objectives.

Many students end up doing TV public service spots locally, by persuading local social agencies to pay only for the production costs. What the students don't gain in dollars, they gain in experience — and earn a degree of professional status, for what they produce is aired, and can be highlighted in their resumé and added to their work portfolio. Some, on the other hand, have earned good money. For example, Liz sent her proposal to a county chapter of the Massachusetts Medical Society. After a phone interview, she was asked to meet with their board. After the meeting she was handed a check for several thousand dollars and asked to produce the spot she had proposed. What was produced was so effective, that she was asked to do five more spots for $20,000. They were done the summer following her last semester at STCC.

Writing a 30-minute drama is a tremendous confidence builder; so much so that it has inspired some students, who did poorly in high school English, to become writers. I have never become jaded observing their struggle, which starts with fear and ends with joy. I can identify with how they feel when they hand in their final draft; it's given to me like a mother handing over her baby. I view my role in their writing a television drama as a combination of cheerleader and coach. I create an optimistic atmosphere, chart the way, reveal the dramatic form to follow and share what elements are necessary to produce an appealing script. We use a step-by-step approach. The first week they write a 30- to 60-second opening, which is critiqued by me and the rest of the class. A week later, they're expected to write three minutes of script, following the opening. Five minutes is due the following week. This process goes on for eight weeks, with a class critiquing every time we meet. Interestingly, most students find their peer group consultations, which are done off campus, more productive than the formal class critiquing sessions. What impresses me is how seriously the students take these get-togethers, which require absolutely no supervision on my part.

One of the reasons why the consultations work so well is that the students know what they're doing. Their knowledge comes from another course they're taking the same semester — "Analysis of Commercial and Public TV." In that course they learn how to critique, by applying an analysis format to TV programs they're assigned to watch. Prior to a thorough explanation of how to use the format, I point out what they can gain from mastering the analysis technique they'll be using. I have learned that all of our students, regardless of background, do better work when they know what personal benefits they can derive from a new learning method I'm about to introduce. I try to give those talks with conviction and enthusiasm and, when appropriate, I'll explain how I personally benefited from the method.

The format is simple. There are four sections. The first one is a succinct description of the program, with information on when it was aired, its length, on what station it was shown, and the nature of the show. In describing the latter, the student must identify the program's theme, plot, all of the subplots, and the moral, if there is one. The second and third sections are similar. Though the approach is the same, the intent is different. In the second one, the student identifies the positive aspects of the show in terms of direction, acting, writing, editing, camera work, lighting, and any other technical production aspect. The negative aspects are identified in the third section.

Most students have no trouble identifying what they think is good and bad, but they struggle with qualifying their generalizations. Because I stress qualification over and over, often pointing out why and how learning to qualify generalizations will help them get ahead professionally — most students eventually overcome this shortcoming. They use examples in the show to support their claims. By the end of the semester, they find themselves becoming more objective. Even their friends and parents notice the change, which can become an irritant when watching television together. Though most of our students have had that experience, none — as far as I know — has been hit by a flying soda bottle.

The fourth section strengthens the students' atrophying creative muscles — caused by excessive TV watching. According to Marshall McCluhan, the late communications prophet/philosopher, television becomes our imagination when we watch it. In the fourth section, students have to explain how to improve what they find wrong with the show. If there's trouble with the script, they attempt to rewrite the portion or portions they don't like. To take what they are doing in class out of the realm of abstraction, I encourage our students to send their critiques to the producers of the shows they have analyzed. None of our students has received a job offer, but they have received letters of encouragement, which have been confidence boosters. And they have been drawn into the professional world.

We do more than critique programs in this course. Every two weeks we hold debates on pressing television issues — for example, the nationalization of American broadcasting television, or abolishing violence on TV, or the reinstatement of cigarette ads on television. The students are divided into A and B sections. Each side is given an opposing view. Often a student defends a view he has always opposed. Though he balks at first, in time he learns to appreciate the benefits derived from the exercise: his sense of objectivity heightens and he grows more tolerant, for, in researching the issue, he may discover something that changes his view. But even if his mind isn't changed, he's expected to argue forcefully for the position he must defend. Later in the semester I ask them to switch positions in mid-debate, to sharpen their thinking processes.

Now, the debate is not a free-for-all. Everyone must prepare a brief, and be prepared to read it in class. I call on five or six people on each side to share what they have written. While this is going on students are taking notes, preparing for the open-ended rebuttal, which is usually free spirited. And I prefer it that way. Their excitement generates enthusiasm for thinking, for learning. There are times when they don't want to stop debating, focusing their wrath on me for calling it quits. Interestingly, they generate a high level of excitement even though there's no declared winner. It is the means they learn to appreciate more than the end, an attitude they'll find far more useful in the work world than winning a class debate.

The students' genuine commitment to the debate aspect of the course became evident to me one day several years ago when, much to my regret, I showed up late to class because a bad snowfall during the night had made driving hazardous. They had started without me. In fact, they were so involved in the debate they didn't take time to heckle me for breaking one of my sacred rules. For an hour, I was just an observer. The students had chosen one of their classmates to replace me as moderator.

In "Advanced TV Journalism" — the last course our students take with me — I do very little teaching. They produce a 30-minute TV newscast for the college community, covering world, national, state, local and campus news, as well as sports, and weather — and they do features. I have no say in the editorial process and technical production of the program. They are on their own. While they're hammering out the newscast, I'm in my office, which adjoins the newsroom, available only if there's a technical or logistical emergency. In a sense, I function as a consultant. After viewing and critiquing the program, I gather the staff together, sharing what I liked and disliked; of course always qualifying my generalizations. They have the option of embracing my recommendations, adopting some aspects of them or rejecting them.

Some superficial observers may charge that I have relinquished control, which could lead to classroom chaos. Actually, it isn't a case of me giving up my authority; it's rather a brilliant display of student self-control. For three semesters our students have been conditioned to respect and internalize that quality. And in doing the newscast they have a semester-long opportunity to exercise it. In the fifteen years I've "taught" the course, there's never been a serious breakdown in the newscast procedure — a student revolt or mass abandonment of duties. When a person complained to our division chairman that I wasn't present in the classroom while the students were preparing the newscast, I was asked to explain my unorthodox behavior. Fortunately, the division head was tolerant of my unusual teaching style. He didn't understand it, but he tolerated it, because he was a result-oriented person. Our department had a solid record. After listening to my explanation, he accepted it but, I'm sure, with reservations. Those doubts vanished, however, when he took a visiting professor from a different college to observe our students putting the newscast together. The visitor expressed amazement at our students' dedication to their tasks, their enthusiasm, and level-headedness in the face of extreme pressure.

The students' ability to produce the newscast is based on what they learned in an intensive TV journalism course they took the previous semester. It actually prepares them to produce the newscast. Near the end of that course, the framework of the program is established — and the staff is put together. The producer, who's in charge, is chosen by his classmates via a secret ballot election. And he appoints the editors of all the news coverage units, which employ consultation to arrive at decisions. The producer also selects the director, who chooses the technical staff. Every student, other than the producer, is a member of a news unit and must write at least two stories. I'm aware of what each student is doing, because the producer files a report with me after each newscast. In that report he evaluates the performance of every staff member, indicating who did well and who was absent, late and uncooperative, and why. A copy of the script and the unused written stories are included, which I scrutinize. Everyone is aware of the report — and my interest in it.

The newscast fulfills a number of functions: it is a means of expressing what the students have learned in TV journalism; it's an opportunity to operate in professional-like conditions; it's a community service; and it's a chance to put into practice all of the things they learned in my classes and the technical courses taken with my departmental colleague, Kirk Smallman.

Kirk joined our department at the start of my second year at STCC. Our fourteen-year professional relationship has been outstanding. I know it's hard to believe, but we have never had a disagreement, not even a minor one. And our students benefit from the unity of purpose that we manifest. Both of us put the interest of the students ahead of everything else, and they know that. They also know that we have a deep respect for one another, for they'll hear me praise Kirk for what he's done professionally, and they'll hear Kirk say positive things about me. It isn't something we plan; it's simply a case of our mutual respect surfacing naturally. Without being plagued by faculty backbiting, character assassination and power-base building, our department has a secure learning environment. Consequently, many students like to stay around after class to discuss television communications or do something extra in the studio.

Considering our personalities, academic backgrounds and aptitudes, Kirk and I should be continually at odds with one another. While he's naturally analytical, methodical, precise and has a Ph.D., I'm naturally intuitive, impulsive, a quick creator of ideas, with only a Bachelor's degree. I think our respect for one another is based on an appreciation of what we do best, and an awareness of how those qualities, and our combined knowledge, can help students. But that's not all. Being honest with one another — and ourselves — has allowed us to appreciate what we do best. We're aware of our strengths and weaknesses as teachers. For example, I've told him about my aversion toward mechanical things — so he teaches the technical courses, which he loves doing. Though I'm a plumber's son, I wouldn't try fixing a leaky faucet. I'm one of those guys who breaks out in a sweat when he has to bang a nail into a wall. My mechanical ineptness has become a departmental joke. Since Kirk has difficulty sorting out a student's stumbling-blocks to learning, he leaves that to me.

Though I've been department chairman for fourteen years, we have always operated as equal partners, with each one handling those things he does best. When Kirk took over as chairman in 1988, the department's division of labor didn't change. As for my strange teaching style, that doesn't phase him at all. While he doesn't employ my approach — and I would never insist that he do — he supports what I do because he knows that it helps our students. In fact, he doesn't mind when I show up at the start of one of his classes to lead the students in their class song.

In searching for a faculty member back in 1974, I wanted someone with a strong practical background in media communications, who would base his curriculum on what he has done in the field. Not only that, he would have to like teaching, be unselfish enough to put his students' interests ahead of his own, and have integrity. I found all of that in Kirk. When I hired him, I knew intuitively that I had made the right choice. What I didn't know at the time was how the two of us, as a team, would provide our students with a balanced education.

As you can tell, I rely heavily on intuition as a teacher. Anyone who never uses a lesson plan would have to. True, I had developed a TV communications department curriculum for Dean Dunn. While it officially remains the teaching framework for our department, what is taught is continually being changed. The changes are based on the needs of the students; and the needs are determined by getting to know the students through personal discussions and their performance in class, especially the essays they prepare for "Communicating in Today's World."

I employ a right-brained approach. In other words, I'm more concerned with the whole than the parts. Process is stressed over facts. I believe the whole determines the behavior of the parts and not the other way around.

When I started teaching at STCC, I had no idea that I would have students writing a textbook and a 30-minute TV drama or producing a proposal for a public service spot. I needed vehicles to teach process and through a flash of inspiration they came into being. When our students complete their textbook, they have experienced an important process, which they can employ in the future. And because they have already done it, they won't be afraid of employing it again. Writing a book is no longer a mystery; it is something they have internalized. As far as I'm concerned the experience of writing the book is far more important than the facts students learn in putting it together. My conviction is based on personal experience. Remember my ordeal in preparing a plan for the America's Cup coverage? At the time I had never developed a TV coverage plan and knew nothing about yachting. I plunged into the assignment with trepidation. But I did it; and only after doing it, I figured out what I had done, and can now articulate the process clearly.

PART TWO

A New Educational
Paradigm for a New Age

CHAPTER
TEN

Nurturing the Unborn Child

The human being is an extremely adaptable creature. If, for example, he has to live in a cave, his survival instincts would most likely force him to survey the life-sustaining resources that are available in his surroundings, cultivate them, and construct a way of life that could bring him a degree of contentment. His adjustment to what others may view as a very limited life style can become so deeply rooted that he resists tenaciously all attempts to change his ways. And it doesn't matter that he's ignorant of the world beyond the cave and the vast opportunities that exist for him to grow spiritually and intellectually. He's determined to stay where he is, inexorably attached to what is familiar and seemingly safe.

In many ways, formal education today maintains the kind of caveman mentality just described. It resists any attempt to alter its established view of what education is, and when it should begin. Kindergarten is the traditional and widely accepted starting point. This remains the case despite the uncovering of more and more scientific evidence that learning begins before the age of five. The long held pedagogical view that a human being is born "a clean slate," that his development is dependent solely on environmental influences after birth, has been debunked. While environment plays an important role in human development, heredity is also a major factor. Moreover, now scientists have unearthed evidence that human behavior, intelligence and personality are being developed prior to birth — while in the mother's womb. We are discovering, for example, youngsters exposed to the violin on a regular basis during gestation have a yearning to play the instrument as a child. A mother who manages to remain calm throughout pregnancy stands a good chance of delivering a calm baby, whereas an anxiety-ridden mother may produce an anxiety-ridden child. A pregnant woman's emotional state may be transferred to the child she's carrying. Toronto psychiatrist Thomas Verny, a well known researcher in prenatal development, has collected scores of accounts of how child behavior is shaped by an expectant mother's interaction with the life within her. One mother, he points out, recalled a Peter, Paul and Mary song she had sung repeatedly during her pregnancy. After the birth of her child, that song had a magical effect on the infant: no matter how hard he was crying, whenever his mother started singing that song — and that song alone — he would quiet down.

Dr. Verny has begun to help parents establish two-way communication between the outside world and the womb. By singing and talking to the fetus, parents create a positive womb environment, reducing the level of anxiety-producing hormones that lead to frenetic activity and even ulcers in the unborn. In his exploration of the unborn child, Verny has learned that by the fourth month after conception it has a well developed sense of touch and taste. At the same age, the baby could perceive a bright light shining on the mother's abdomen; if the light was particularly bright, the fetus would even lift his hands to shield his eyes. At five months the same unborn child would react to loud sounds by raising his hands and covering his ears. According to University of North Carolina psychologist Anthony DeCasper an embryo begins to recognize speech sounds about six and a half weeks before birth. Consequently, a newborn recognizes his mother's voice. Other researchers have gone even further, creating stimulation systems based on language, touch, and heart rhythm. When transmitted to the place where a human embryo resides, researchers claim, these stimuli improve an individual's ability to learn. Neuroscientist Dominick Purpura discovered in one of his studies at New York's Albert Einstein Medical College that the human cerebral cortex — the seat of thought — forms the structure necessary for learning sometime between the twenty-eighth and thirty-second weeks of pregnancy.

While more and more evidence is being unearthed concerning the fetus' ability to respond to its environment, there are people — often considered backward — who have been practicing prenatal education for centuries. Those Sioux Indian women who still cling to the "old ways" know what to do when they first feel the flicker of life within them: it's a signal to adopt a prayerful attitude, to be calm, to live in a tranquil setting, to think noble thoughts, to beseech the Great Spirit to make her child strong, a person of fine character, a lover of all life, and a kind and wise human being. She'll stand before a waterfall for long periods of time in order to expose the life within her to beauty. There's no question in her mind that such exposure is enriching her unborn baby.

Her husband assists by creating a peaceful environment, trying always to keep his wife from becoming depressed, frustrated and fearful. For he, too, knows instinctively that the life that he helped to conceive is affected by his wife's feelings and thoughts. And he makes sure that she eats and drinks only nutritious foods, for they both know that what a mother consumes is shared with the life within her.

Unfortunately, the great majority of Sioux women have abandoned their ancient cultural ways for the "white man's ways," including alcohol consumption, the result being a scourge of alcoholism sweeping through Indian communities in North America. Anthropologist Michael Dorris — half Indian himself — who is tracking this social disaster, knows that women who drink heavily can produce mental retardation, curvature of the spine and facial abnormalities in the fetus; even a moderate or small amount of drinking may produce a child with emotional problems, insomnia, and a chronic inability to cope in school and on the job. In his book, *The Broken Cord*, Dr. Dorris asks the operative question, "If you wouldn't give your kid a bottle of gin the day after birth, why give it one the day before?"

When the prevailing educational systems were established, neuroscientists weren't trying to find out whether a fetus could learn. Science had no inclination to probe in that direction. Most educators at the time were convinced that humans were born a "clean slate," that professional teachers had the sole responsibility of educating children; and that education started at age five. It's been that way for more than 100 years. I know that changing long established practices is difficult. Historically, there's been opposition to new ideas, even ideas that one day proved beneficial to humankind. Scientists and philosophers were persecuted for expounding ideas that ran counter to the entrenched view. We know what Socrates and Galileo had to endure.

The findings of Verny, DeCasper and Purpura challenge the education community at a time when the prevailing pedagogy is failing, when society's moral and spiritual underpinnings are collapsing. Bold initiatives are needed in educating those who'll determine the destiny of our nation, our planet. When I think of how ignorant most parents are of their prenatal care responsibilities, I am saddened for the millions of unborn children. They will be born deprived of the kind of start in life Nature meant them to have. Living in a society that's obsessed with personal gain and pleasure, many pregnant women — rich and poor — pay little attention to the life within them, many feeling sorry for themselves for having to bear a child, considering it both an economic and physical burden. With teenage pregnancy on the rise, we even find junior high school and high school girls without the support of a husband, unable to afford proper prenatal medical care, and woefully ignorant of the need to educate their unborn child. And what about the increasing number of pregnant alcoholics and cocaine and heroin addicts? What chance will their offspring have to live secure and happy lives?

When I think of the young drug pusher, the bigot, the terrorist, the addict sniffing cocaine; when I think of the hordes of Hell's Angels armed with chains and clubs roaring into town, I can't help but wonder how they would have turned out if their parents had consciously showered them with love while in the womb; if their parents had consciously exposed them to beauty, wisdom and the power of the Divine Reality. The fetus within a pregnant woman is more than an unconscious growing blob of protoplasm, as many expectant parents believe. To assure a healthy beginning in life, it needs the kind of loving care a seed gets from a conscientious gardener. Should more humans awaken to the fact that human development starts before birth; that parenthood and education begin when a woman and a man learn that they have conceived life, and they take seriously the responsibility of properly educating the fetus — chances are that brighter, more secure, emotionally healthier and more altruistic human beings will be produced, creating a saner, much less violent, more cooperative and compassionate world.

I believe there is a correlation between the mounting racism, drug use, violence, emotional instability, moral degradation, self-hate — and the present day parents' ignorance of the need to educate their unborn child. School systems need to expand their services to include the training of prospective and potential parents on how to be effective prenatal educators.

CHAPTER
ELEVEN

Parents as Educators

Obviously, if parents are to be involved in nurturing their unborn child, they certainly must continue their educational efforts after the baby is born. Learning is going on when the mother first embraces her infant. While the learning experience has nothing to do with mathematics or history, the love received from the mother is helping to create a secure emotional foundation in the child. Children without such a foundation often have trouble developing intellectually. I often wonder what would have happened to me if my poorly educated mother hadn't continually showered love upon me. Her awareness of the need to love her baby wasn't spawned from a book; it was instinctual. I'm sure that had she known what my wife knows about human nature and development, her children would have benefited a lot more from their childhood experiences. For instance, while my mother sensed that humans needed love, she was unaware of the inherent human yearning to know, and consequently did very little to satisfy that natural desire in her children, or herself. Neither my mother nor my father ever read to us or took us to the library; they never engaged us in intellectually stimulating conversations.

We grew up knowing that we couldn't receive satisfactory answers from our parents concerning questions like — what makes the sun shine? or, how does a bird fly? And because they had little understanding of the human being's spiritual dimension, their children approached adulthood practically devoid of any spiritual development. Reality to us was simply what we could see, feel, smell and hear. It didn't matter that we went to synagogue on the high holy days, and that I went through the Bar Mitzvah ritual. I had absolutely no understanding of my spirit; that, like my body, it needed development for me to be a truly healthy human being. Later in the book when I focus on moral education a fairly full explanation will be given of the human being's spiritual nature (see Chapter 14).

Really, parents are a child's first teachers. Unfortunately, most aren't aware that whatever they do in the presence of their children is being absorbed by them — the good and bad. I'm sure my father had no intention of inculcating within me a deep dislike of any kind of mechanical involvement. But that's what happened, even though he tried to create the opposite effect. He taught me to fear doing mechanical things by the way he reacted when I made a mistake while helping him fix something. He would shout, call me names and sometimes shove me. My phobia got so bad that whenever my father ordered me to assist him in one of his mechanical projects I made up excuses why I couldn't heed the order. I'd prefer being spanked than being humiliated. To this day whenever I'm confronted by a mechanical responsibility my mind locks up, I become fearful, remembering the emotional rejection and physical pain contained in the first incident with my father.

While parents are the child's first teachers, mothers have the most influence because, since they tend to spend more time with their children, a special bond develops between them. There is also the biological factor. But a child's education must continue beyond that stage. Actually, a human being's education is meant to be ongoing, never-ending. Schooling, which is only a short educational phase, should inspire humans to gain more knowledge after graduation and prepare them to secure it on their own.

To educate properly, parents must take a holistic approach. While helping to build a solid cognitive foundation in their child, they're also responsible for guiding the development of the youngster's character, to the extent that he is gaining an accurate understanding of what a human being is and what the purpose of life is, feels good about himself, has an appreciation for order and discipline, a working understanding of such behavioral principles and standards as courtesy, truthfulness, thoughtfulness, cooperation, promptness, the need to finish what you start, and a sincere willingness to help others. I'm sure you can add much more to the list.

Discovering their child's potentialities is one of the most important teaching responsibilities of parents. When that's being done, the youngster begins to gain an understanding of who he really is. With such self-knowledge, a child starts to feel good about himself — which generates internal strength and security. Instead of directing his energy and attention on his ineptness and insecurities, he's enthusiastically focused on the world outside of himself, exploring it and experiencing a sense of fulfillment through his discoveries.

My wife has a special knack for discovering potential in children. She did a good job with ours. When our youngest son Tod was two, he would throw terrible temper tantrums. We didn't know what to make of it. Slugging him wasn't going to solve the problem, although there were moments when I had to steel myself from carrying out my animalistic urge. Carol found the solution. Considering herself our children's first educator, she scrutinized them for signs of potential. One day she noticed how involved Tod was while drawing a picture; he was deeply into his own world. And what he was drawing was outstanding for his age — no stick figures. He was doing three dimensional renderings of children. That was a signal to Carol that she had to nurture her son's artistic potential. It was also a sign to both of us that his screaming was his way of expressing a need for creative fulfillment.

Had I followed my impulse to belt him, I would not only have forced him to repress a natural yearning, but he would have learned to resent me and to resort to violence in resolving conflicts with others. The notion that parents should let their children cry for long periods of time in order to prevent them from being spoiled is a misguided notion popularized by certain eminent physicians and psychologists in the 1930s, 40s and 50s. When a baby cries, he needs something. Often parents lack the patience or wisdom to discover their baby's need. Carol gave Tod what he needed. She provided him with crayons, paper, paints. She brought home books from the library with paintings of the Masters. She read to him about some of the great artists, took him to museums, suggested pictures he should copy, and encouraged him to draw and paint what he wanted to draw and paint. She critiqued his paintings, offering suggestions on how he could improve his work. They developed a trust for one another that is now the basis of a close and healthy relationship. Tod not only conquered his tendency toward temper tantrums, but today he's basically a calm and secure human being.

Carol's ability to identify potential has rubbed off on me. When my son David and his family spent several weeks with us, I noticed his two-year-old son Evan demonstrating a fascination for music. Unlike our other grandchildren he didn't bang on our piano when he sat before it; his little fingers ran reverently over the keys. Shortly before he and his family returned home, we all went to a fancy wedding in Boston together. It was a hot day, and Evan took off his shoes and socks, unbuttoned his shirt, walked over to the musicians, stretched out at the foot of the violinist, with his eyes half closed, delighting over Bach, Mozart and Chopin.

When I shared my observations with Evan's mother and father, they pointed out that they had noticed the same thing about their youngest child and were planning to develop his musical potential. The fact that they were aware cheered my heart, because they were taking seriously their role as their children's first teachers. Watching my other daughter-in-law, Greta, feed her five-month-old son also cheered my heart — and taught me a lot. She was feeding him more than cereal, carrots and applesauce. Though I was sitting about six feet away from her, she seemed oblivious of me. Greta was completely focused on her baby, and though he couldn't speak, I could tell that he was appreciative of the attention, for his big brown eyes were trained on his mother. Normally a physically active child, he sat quietly, in a near trance. He could feel his mother's love, and I sensed that in his own primitive way he was reciprocating.

But there was more than an exchange of love. While feeding little Zachary, his mother kept talking to him as if he understood everything she was saying. It was no gushy baby-talk. On the other hand, it was not a series of matter-of-fact messages. There was love and respect in her voice. Yes, respect! Greta acknowledged her infant's humanness by acknowledging his feelings. When he tasted the carrots and cringed, she said to him, "I see you don't like the carrots as much as you like applesauce, but you have to eat the carrots, because its going to help you grow strong." While Zachary continued to cringe when his mother fed him carrots, he didn't reject them. Greta's conversation with her five-month-old child was achieving another purpose. She was helping him develop a sound speech pattern. Her three-year-old son Alex has been the beneficiary of this process. He started speaking in complete sentences at eighteen months and has an extraordinary vocabulary. He also loves books. His passion for books is the result of his parents reading to him regularly ever since he was an infant. Shortly after supper, Greta read Zachary a story and placed the little book in the child's hands.

Our children have profited from their parents' involvement in their education. The three sons who have completed college are pursuing careers in professions that fascinate them, and our daughter, who's in her last year of college, and who has a solid understanding of her potential, is charting a career course that'll be personally fulfilling. But what impresses my wife and me most is our children's genuine desire to be of service to others, to make people happy, to do as much as possible to make this world a better place.

I have mentioned my children not to create an opportunity to beam with fatherly pride, but to provide an example, that I have been extremely close to, of what can result from conscientious and sensitive parental guidance in the education of one's children, especially during their preschool years. It wasn't easy. But then again no worthwhile creative effort is.

When other parents would ask Carol for her special formula, she would respond by saying, "Constant worry." My interpretation of her comment is that she was always concerned about our children's development. I don't think that in our 35-year marriage we missed a day reviewing the development of our three sons and daughter — and we still do, but in a different way. While we respect their privacy, our children know that we can be tapped for assistance, if need be. And there are times when my wife takes the initiative when she knows her children are faced with a difficult problem, one that they have shared with us. For example, when two of our sons and daughters-in-law moved overseas, they expressed some concern about their children's education. Carol's reaction was to research home teaching techniques. She read books, contacted learning institutes, interviewed educators. After sifting through mounds of information — and learning a lot through the process — she shared her findings with our sons and daughters-in-law who needed help. Both young families are using what they received from Carol — and their children are benefiting from it.

As you can tell, Carol's "constant worry" isn't a negative reflex that leads to sulking and inaction. It is a stimulus to do something constructive. What drives her to be an effective parent/teacher? A deep desire to be faithful to her religion's teachings on parenting. It is something I have taken to heart as well — thanks to Carol's lead. Of course being conscientious doesn't mean that our efforts were always free of hardship, frustration and anguish. There were even times of self-pity, when we wanted to do something personally fulfilling instead of interacting with our children. There were those low moments! Even moments when we succumbed to the temptation of putting our interests ahead of our children's.

Our saving grace was that we knew what we were doing and what the consequences would be. It wasn't only the fear of displeasing God that prompted us to get back on the proper parental track; it was also a deep awareness of how influential our attitude and behavior was in the development of our children's present and future lives. We understood that what we did and said — even our moods — could affect our children.

This doesn't mean that we didn't make mistakes, get angry and "blow up" from time to time. What helped was that when something like that would happen in our children's presence, we would usually acknowledge our poor behavior, explaining why we were angry or had lost our temper — and would apologize. Now it's important to point out that the kind of response I have just mentioned was less apparent during the early years of my child-rearing duties.

Carol was far more conscious of her parental responsibilities than I was. Thank God for that! In those days, most of my energy went into establishing a secure professional career. Oh, I had read some of the material Carol had given me concerning the father's role in a child's development. It took a deeply emotional and painful experience for me to internalize the stuff I had read. One day I blew up at one of my sons — who was six or seven at the time. He had interrupted me while I was engrossed in an important work project that I was having difficulty organizing. I resented the interruption. All he wanted was for me to pull out the whistle from a cereal box. Enraged, I cried out, "fool!" and struck the child hard on his arm, knocking the box out of his hands, and crushing it with my foot. I'll never forget my son's reaction. He didn't wail. He stood before me in stunned disbelief, tears streaming down his cheeks. My heart aching, and crying, I embraced the little boy, whispering, "I'm sorry. I'm sorry." As I cradled him in my arms I reflected on how I could have done such a thing. I had never struck any of my children before.

What I found disturbing was that I had reacted the way my father reacted whenever I would cross him as a child. In fact, in reviewing what I had said and done, I realized that I had used the word that my father often directed at me, and like him, I had carried my anger to an extreme. There was the time, when after hitting me, he smashed my toy truck with his foot. I had done practically the very same thing to my child. Evidently, it didn't matter that I detested my father whenever he beat me. Somehow his raging behavior was absorbed by me and became a part of my behavioral pattern. My father, whom I loved, had taught me to hate. When he blew up, he would come after me with the same kind of home-made whip that his father beat him with. Yet I know my father didn't hate me; there had been tender moments between us. His idea of bringing up children was shaped by the way he was brought up. He didn't know any better.

My sense is that the upsurge in violence in America and elsewhere can be traced to homes where children were treated violently by their parents. In her book, *For Your Own Good*, Swiss psychotherapist Alice Miller explores the life of Adolf Hitler — perhaps history's most monstrous mass murderer — to reveal the cause of his all-consuming hatred. She points out that young Adolf was beaten every day of his childhood by an insecure father, plagued by self-hatred, and who himself had been beaten regularly as a child. Miller points out that the future Nazi Führer's greatest pleasure came from defying his father by forcing himself not to utter a sound while being pummeled. While Adolf Hitler had no children, he found a way of unleashing his repressed hatred and utilizing the violent behavior he had learned as a child. By citing Hitler's horrific childhood, I don't mean to convey that every child that's beaten by his parents will end up doing what Hitler did. But the chances are great that the battered child will beat his children when he becomes a parent. Most American prison convicts who committed violent crimes came from homes where violence was used to resolve conflicts and overcome frustration. Or they came from homes where the husband and wife psychologically abdicated their roles as parents, allowing television to become the third — and most influential — parent in the home.

Violence breeds violence. Even Hitler wasn't born a violent person, a hater. That was drummed into him by parents who were ignorant of their responsibilities as educators of their children. They needed help, as did many other parents in the late 1800s who subscribed to the popular "Spare the rod and spoil the child" child-rearing philosophy.

And today's parents need help, too. In some respects the need is greater now than in the past. With more people around, there are more crimes, which create serious problems like a shortage of jail space. But building new prisons is a "band-aid"

solution. What's needed is to create the means of preventing
children from pursuing the path of crime. Parents are in a
position to do that, as well as to guide their sons and daughters
to become caring and civil and productive citizens in society.
But to accomplish that they need to know, first, that they are
responsible for the beginning phase of their children's education;
and are willing to gain the knowledge required to be an effective
first teacher of their children. While a few highly motivated,
open-minded and financially secure parents will take on the
responsibilities, most won't for economic and philosophical
reasons, or sheer lack of interest.

A government-financed educational campaign designed to
persuade parents to take an active role in their children's
education is needed. Professional teachers shouldn't feel
threatened by such an undertaking; in fact they should support
it, if not for humanitarian reasons, then for selfish reasons.
There'll be more teaching jobs, for parents will have to be
trained to be teachers of their preschoolers; and colleges of
education will have to expand their services to train the teachers
of parents. Unfortunately, what I'm suggesting runs counter to
the existing established social, economic and political patterns in
most nations. Take, for instance, the United States of America.
The great outcry for reform in formal education isn't motivated
by a desire to help youngsters discover, release and develop their
potential, to help them grow into secure, happy, service-oriented
human beings — lovers of knowledge who derive pleasure from
the process of gaining it.

The main reason why pressure for reform has intensified on
the federal level is the realization that the quality of the
American worker pool is deteriorating. There is a 25% school
dropout rate. And many who manage to graduate are considered
functionally illiterate. These are young men and women without
even potential work skills, who cannot qualify for manufacturing
type jobs, let alone jobs in the high tech industries that must
prosper if the U.S.A. is to remain competitive with countries like
Japan, Germany, South Korea. Corporations are crying out for
help. And while governmental leaders are trying to find who to
blame for the sorry educational condition, they are puzzled as to

what went wrong. After all, they state, Americans spend more money on education than any other country in the world — more than 300 billion dollars last year. The trouble is that most of that money has been funneled into elementary, junior high school, high school and college education. Only a minute amount has gone into educating preschoolers. The major problem facing education in America is not the failing school system — though that's a real problem, and deserves serious attention. Ignorance of the need to educate humans before they start school is the major problem. The shaping of a dropout begins long before he reaches high school. The same is true of most criminals.

CHAPTER
TWELVE

The Vital Preschool Years

Unfortunately, there's a controversy raging over the value of teaching preschoolers to read, write, do mathematics and play the violin. Many highly respected pedagogists cringe at the idea of teaching preschoolers what's taught in schools, because they believe the children are too immature to appreciate what they're supposed to be learning. These educators charge that forcing intellectual maturity upon children could damage them psychologically. Every human being needs a full childhood experience, they believe. The first five years of life, they contend, should be devoted to developing a child's character, concentrating on building self-esteem, confidence, a strong moral foundation and a feel for community service. They also fear that early intellectual development will eventually retard a student's interest in school, causing "academic burnout" in high school and college. And some opponents to early home learning also cite incidents of social-status-conscious parents subjecting their infants to force-feeding educational programs in order to impress neighbors and friends with their toddler's brilliance — and to assure his admittance into Harvard.

These are valid concerns. On the other hand, those who own these concerns are being challenged by new scientific findings regarding early childhood learning capabilities.

Neuroscientists are uncovering evidence that the greatest opportunity for some kinds of intellectual development is between infancy and six. It seems that during this sensitive period of time the human brain is most susceptible to acquiring certain basic intellectual skills like language, reading, writing, and mathematics — skills that make up the springboard for more advanced intellectual development. What's necessary is the stimulus to set off the learning process. If no conscious effort is made to provide the proper stimulation, the child will be deprived of taking advantage of a once-in-a-lifetime opportunity to make great strides in its intellectual growth.

Our children's brains grow as much as we give them the chance to grow. Most neurophysiologists agree that the more you use your brain the more it'll grow, and therefore the better it will perform. But they warn that what we don't use we lose. In a way, it's like a former athlete whose muscles weaken, even atrophy from non-use. In other words, function determines structure. For example, studies done on animals show that when deprived of light at an early age, over an extended period of time, they become blind. Eyes, like other organs, are meant to be used. And the brain is an organ. Neurophysiologists point out that in its first six years, the human brain takes in facts at lightning speed. This happens because the brain is in the period of its greatest development, when it is more pliable, and most naturally desirous of nourishment.

In a way, it's like the period of time when the human being is experiencing his greatest general physical growth — at that time, he craves food and stimulation. In like manner, the preschooler, including the infant, craves mental nourishment. When parents deprive their two-, three-, and four-year-olds of this nourishment, allowing their children to get it haphazardly from external forces like television, radio and their friends who are being brought up in a similar environment, the youngsters will most likely evolve into dull adults. The more consistent a parent is in nourishing her child's brain during this critical period, the brighter her child will be. Geniuses, for the most part, are made, not born. If Albert Einstein, for example, had been confined to a windowless and unlit room for the first thirteen years of life, he would have been an idiot, but obviously his young brain had been properly nourished. Tragically, most parents are unaware of the power they have to help their child discover and develop her genius.

One sign of a toddler's genius is his ability to learn a language between birth and 36 months. In fact, if a child grows up in a home where two or three languages are spoken, he speaks two or three languages; by age six, he's speaking them perfectly, and is able to use them interchangeably — while an adult usually struggles to learn a language. No mystery. All significant brain growth is completed by age six. The magical critical period has passed. In the words of Harvard's Dr. Howard Gardner, a leading human developmentalist: "During such critical periods it is crucial for the organism to inhabit a properly enriched environment where it can partake of relevant sensory experiences and activities. Rearing during this period in an impoverished environment or one deficient in proper triggers [stimulation] can have a deleterious long term effect" (Howard Gardner, "Notes on Cognitive Development: Recent Trends, Common New Directions," in S. Freidman (et al), *The Brain, Cognition and Education*, New York, NY: Academic Press, 1986, p. 259). The late pedagogical pioneer Dr. Maria Montessori, who observed early childhood development for years, was aware of this critical learning period in human development: "Children pass through definite periods in which they reveal psychic aptitudes and possibilities which afterwards disappear. That is why at particular epochs of their life, they reveal an intense and extraordinary interest in certain objects and exercises, which one might look for in vain at a later age" (E.M. Standing, *Maria Montessori: Her Life and Work*. New York, NY: Mentor Books, 1962).

Shiniki Suzuki's knowledge of this critical learning period has been put to good use in helping two- and three-year-olds learn the language of music. Suzuki has taught directly and indirectly 100,000 tiny children around the world to play the violin. Interestingly, his mission is not to create world famous concert virtuosos but, rather, to build up toddlers' intelligence and assist in their development as better human beings. He believes there is linkage between intelligence and memory — and that the best time to develop one's memory capacity is during the sensitive periods in the brain's development. With an early developed memory bank, it is much easier to learn to read. Suzuki has two- and three-year-olds memorize sheet music one day and play the score by heart the next day. An adult would have difficulty doing that. Again, after age six all significant brain growth has ended.

What's amazing is that holistic educators have noticed two-year-olds learn to read without being subjected to the phonics method. The children discover the rules of phonics without being exposed to them. This right-brain activity also allows preschoolers to perceive quantity without counting. For example, three-year-olds, receiving a regular dose of brain stimulation and nourishment, have demonstrated the ability to determine the right number of sticks or pennies on the ground without counting them. Apparently, the same law that develops language is in operation when toddlers learn to read and perceive quantity. While we know all preschoolers possess this special latent power, and some educators and parents know how to tap it, its origin and what operationalizes it remains a mystery.

Can we afford to ignore these findings, and continue to apply the antiquated, often crippling, prevailing pedagogical beliefs in educating our children? If the evidence I've cited is true, and we ignore it, wouldn't we be impeding our children's growth, keeping them from realizing their birthright? Now, if the existing educational systems were producing outstanding results, I wouldn't be advocating pre-kindergarten learning. But they're in deep trouble. I feel that disregarding the evidence is like a farmer continuing to plant in May instead of April, even though the latest agricultural research states that breaking with tradition will produce a greater yield. Of course, new scientific breakthroughs and ideas aren't easily accepted, especially if they threaten to change long established patterns of thinking, and of doing things. At one time it was believed that the Earth was flat, and the most respected scholars could prove it through "logical" arguments. This exercise in philosophical manipulation, however, didn't change the reality of our planet's roundness.

My conviction that the evidence I've cited is sound is not only based on what I've read and learned from progressive educators and scholars. I have also been profoundly impressed by the results I have witnessed from my children's and friends' efforts to nourish the developing brains of their preschool sons and daughters.

The fact that attempts to educate preschoolers are based on the wrong motives, and youngsters are emotionally manhandled, doesn't mean we should abandon the opportunity to develop a child's intellect when he's most receptive to certain kinds of learning. What's necessary is a change in teaching approach. Chances are great that a toddler will be abused if a parent pressures him to learn the names of every member of the dinosaur family, and the spelling of twenty three-syllable words — in order to show-off at a dinner party. Motive is all-important. If the parent begins to educate her eighteen-month-old because she wants to take advantage of the best time for her daughter or son to grow intellectually, and employs a loving and kindly approach, the child will respond enthusiastically whenever it's time to learn in an organized setting.

By keeping the "learning time" experience relatively short — no longer than an hour for each child — the children aren't smothered with knowledge, and leave the session wishing it could be longer. Of course, giving them a little information whets their hunger for knowledge and inspires them to search independently for it. It also allows the children lots of time to play, to have a full childhood experience, something critics of organized preschool learning fear most about home learning for toddlers.

In Littleton, Massachusetts, Mehrnoosh Watson has witnessed with delight and gratitude how her four-year-old daughter has grown through the home learning regimen she organized two years ago. Motivated by a profound religious belief that the mother is the first educator of a child, Mehrnoosh engaged in an intensive search for the healthiest way to stimulate her baby's learning capacity. With a strong understanding of human brain development, she sensed that her impulse to nourish her two-year-old's mind was basically sound. What gave her the confidence to proceed was her Faith's (Bahá'í) position on preschool learning, with its emphasis on careful nurturing and educational development from early childhood.

Mehrnoosh was careful not to apply any undue pressure on her daughter, and worked at making the learning experience joyful for the child. Though she was sensitive in her approach, Mehrnoosh was consistent. The first objective was to help her daughter learn to read. Everyday she exposed the child to words printed in large letters on cards — at first, five or six words. She refrained from testing the child, the idea being that the flashed words imprint on the brain when it craves nourishment. In eight months the child was reading on a fourth grade level. And it wasn't a strain, for all it took was a few seconds at a time, several times a day, for a total of 90 seconds. Now, at four, the child is spending an hour a day interacting with her mother. In that time, she writes compositions in complete sentences which are structurally sound, and this has been achieved without being taught grammar. Evidently, a preschooler can learn to write the way she learns to read — the grammar unfolding the way the rules of phonics unfold in the brain.

This phenomenon is based on the principle that preschoolers can't deal with principles. By giving them facts, they seem to deduce the principles naturally. During the "learning hour" the daughter also reads (on a high school level) on a variety of subjects. For example, she can identify many different artists' styles and has developed an appreciation for certain scientific subjects. She also does mathematics and practices the violin. All this without any strain on her. Of course, Mehrnoosh works hard to ensure that her daughter doesn't feel pressured, that she finds the knowledge-enrichment experience exciting and personally rewarding. It seems that the key to her success is stressing process over technique, as she explains:

> Unless one establishes a complete system of patterned interaction with the child, the technique won't work. The quality of the child's response to educational materials has a lot to do with what kind of communications

pattern has been established between parent and child.

A mother, in my opinion, should have confidence in herself and in her child. She not only needs to have a sense of [benign] control of the child, but also to be able to convey to the child a sense of security in her ability to deal with the child. For example, if a mother is uncertain about the appropriate method to discipline her child, the child will sense this ambivalence and will not respond to the mother's efforts. A mother who is not sure about the significance of an educational goal, such as reading, or a method or process by which to accomplish the goal or task, or is not sure of the kind of benefits or dangers which might be present for the child, can very easily convey her uncertainty to her two- or three-year-old child by asking the question, "Do you want to learn your words?" and the two-year-old child whose favorite word is "no", and who senses the anxiety in the mother will say, "no." Finally, the syndrome is completed when the mother, feeling relieved and justified, and yet frustrated says, "My child is not interested in learning to read, so I am not pushing it. The very idea that any two or three-year-old can learn to read must not be a very sound idea after all."

The point is that we can create desires in our children for the things we know are right, and indeed it is our duty to do so. We can do so without creating any pressure on them. It has to be so, or there would be no demand for moral education today. Moreover, just using a technique will not work without a deep understanding behind everything you choose to do because you will always be having to make some choices, and no technique can replace a parent's responsibility to make decisions. Every child is different. Every environment, every circumstance and every experience is different. What is important is to identify the principles and be guided by them. Techniques are most useful if they can be transformed into principles. One must really study a technique in order to achieve the transformation and internalize and effectively practice the results. What I would say to mothers is this: "Mothers, educating our children and watching their flourishing is the most fulfilling, rewarding, joyous occupation we can have. As the song says, 'a child only lasts for a while', and I say 'what we do to a child lasts forever'."

It's sad that so many parents and their children aren't experiencing the bounties that Mehrnoosh and her daughter are experiencing. Is there a greater bounty for parents than to see their little children receive what they naturally crave, to see them grow joyfully, with an excitement for living, and a healthy yearning to know more? When parents see that happening they grow more secure about their little ones' future. Unfortunately, many parents these days are extremely anxious about their children's future because they don't know where to turn for trustworthy help; and there are others who have become so numbed by the struggle to survive from day to day that the future is given little thought. Knowing what I know now, I can't help but wonder about the hundreds of millions of children, especially those stuck in the quicksand of poverty, who are potential geniuses but will never know it. Is there any greater deprivation than that?

Of course, being deprived of organized preschool learning doesn't automatically mean a child will end up hopelessly inept as an adult. I'm sure there are Ph.D.s and corporate presidents who learned to read after age six. What sets them apart from those who received early mental nourishment is that they found schooling, for the most part, more of a chore than a joy. The desire "to amount to something" was a driving force to attain an advanced university degree, or social and economic power, not a passion for the process of acquiring knowledge. Deprived of the opportunity to develop healthy learning habits between birth and six, they developed instead habits that functioned as barriers to school-based learning.

I know what that's like. For example, when I was in school, I wanted answers to questions that intrigued me, but I lacked the will to make the effort to figure them out. Did I reach for books?

Hell, no! Though as a preschooler I was as curious as the next kid, I had been conditioned to obtain information from sources other than the printed word. I turned to radio for knowledge. (There was no public television programming in the 1930s and 40s.) Whenever I would turn the dial and listen, my natural yearning to know was activated — and satisfied to a degree. I didn't enjoy listening to frivolous comedies, even popular ones like the Jack Benny Show; and serials like "The Adventures of Jack Armstrong" and "Captain Midnight" weren't as fascinating to me as public affairs programs like "We the People." Some of my early childhood heroes were news commentators like Raymond Graham Swing, Elmer Davis, Gabriel Heater and H. V. Kaltenborn.

My interest in world affairs was cultivated by a relationship with my maternal grandfather. He often listened to his favorite newscasts with me on his lap. Afterwards he would explain what I had been exposed to. Like him, I rooted for the Loyalists in the Spanish Civil War. I was six at the time. I also remember sitting at the kitchen table with him, pouring over a map and listening to his explanation of how the greatly outnumbered Finnish troops were able to repulse the Soviet invaders. Experiences like that had to be a factor in my developing a deep interest in geography. To this day I'm able to learn faster from conversations and listening to audio tapes than from reading books or articles. And it doesn't matter that I write books and magazine articles. I'm convinced that had I been taught to read prior to entering kindergarten, and my parents demonstrated a love for reading, I wouldn't have grown up with a learning handicap that affected me as a journalist. While I had no trouble covering a story and writing it, or developing and unearthing one, I found rewriting wire service copy difficult. For it required swift reading comprehension ability, something I haven't been able to master — in fact, it remains a struggle.

CHAPTER
THIRTEEN

Individual Uniqueness and Diversity

There's no doubt that if all parents took seriously the challenge to become proficient educators of their preschoolers, the existing public educational institutions would be incapable of properly educating five-year-olds that read on a high school level, can speak one or two foreign languages and solve algebraic problems. Present day educators aren't equipped to educate a legion of geniuses. Their focus has been on preparing students to function effectively in industry or in social service occupations.

But that's not the only reason for the need to restructure formal education. What's desperately needed is a new educational paradigm that's dedicated to discovering, releasing and developing a student's potential and helping him understand what a human being is, who he really is, and what the purpose of life is. If the former is done well, answers to the latter will naturally unfold. Because these three issues aren't addressed in existing school curricula, most students who graduate high school seem fearful of the future, are uncertain about what vocation to pursue and are plagued by insecurity and anxiety, which generate a sense of hopelessness in some. This observation is based on a six year survey I have made at STCC. Of the 205 students I have queried, not one could articulate clearly what a human being is; most of them had never pondered the question. As for the purpose of life? The same results. And most had little idea of their true self. What motivated me to do the survey was an experience I had in an industrial suburb of Liverpool, England, in the summer of 1984.

I was to address the student body of a government sponsored job skills development center; most of them, who had been on welfare for a number of years, were being taught a marketable skill. Interestingly, neither they nor their instructors were optimistic about the students' chances of securing jobs. The gloom was apparent the minute I stepped into the fairly modern facility. In fact, as I mingled with the faculty and students — and they ranged from eighteen-year- olds to sixty-year-olds — I sensed a deep collective depression. There was bitterness and hopelessness etched on their faces. Some of them expressed their resentment toward their condition by painting their faces, wearing rings in their noses and starching and coloring their hair purple and orange. And they had no love for me. In fact, one of the instructors told me, "I wouldn't be surprised if they boot you out of here." I guess they felt that I was a member of the establishment — the enemy who was responsible for their helplessness. Had I come to them with a long beard, wearing a robe and wielding a sword and said "Let's storm the prime minister's residence," all 150 students would have followed me to London.

I didn't know what to say to this group. Originally, I was to speak about religion. But I sensed that these people were fed up with religion, that they were influenced by their Marxist oriented instructors. They were angry and wanted to lash out in the worst way. As I was being introduced, I prayed for guidance. In a few seconds a thought came to mind: speak about what a human being is. And I did. At first they seemed skeptical, and a few interrupted me and challenged me with Marxist dogma. But about half way through my talk, I could see their faces lighting up; the despair in their eyes had been replaced by hope. Brought up to believe that they were fundamentally wicked, they had never been exposed to their inherent beauty and love and their potential for spiritual and intellectual growth. All of their lives they had been caught up in a desperate rhythm of life — like their parents and their grandparents before them. They went to school to learn to read and write and then work in the local factory, get married and have as many children as they could bear, spend most of their leisure time at the pub and root for their favorite football team. That was life! But through my talk they were able to see other possibilities for themselves; they grew excited, keeping me there for four hours, even skipping the 4:00 pm tea time. Reluctantly, I had to break away for I had another commitment that night. I left heavy hearted, because I knew that the next day these people who were able to gain a glimmer of hope would be drawn back into the rhythm of life they were accustomed to — their potential genius unnoticed. Several weeks later while meditating on the experience an interesting thought came to mind: perhaps the students' anger and desire to lash out was a subconscious awareness of being deprived of their birthright to develop the genius within themselves, and they were crying out for help.

Tragically, most American public schools reflect a terrible ignorance of human development, causing the psychological crippling of thousands of human beings. Obviously, the damage isn't done on purpose. It is the way schools are set up to teach that does the damage. A formula approach is used, which has little or no regard for diversity. I'm not referring to cultural diversity, though that must be taken into account as well. I'm referring to the fact that everyone is unique, has his or her own individuality. No two people in the world have the same fingerprints, for example. And every child's home experiences are different. Since no one is exactly alike, not even identical twins, it stands to reason that people learn differently. This became clear as I observed the development of my four children. Though they share some similar interests, they have distinct personalities, talents, and likes and dislikes. My wife and I accepted the differences as an aspect of nature's law of unity in diversity, which recognizes that while all humans come from the same ancestral stock, everyone has a special set of characteristics.

The law of unity in diversity is as real as the law of gravity, and is manifested in every level of life, even among look-alikes. In the mineral world, for example, a sandy beach may appear from the boardwalk as a grey — or beige — colored mass. But when we scoop up a handful of sand and examine each grain, we'll find that each one has its own particular size and shape. Upon close scrutiny we discover that among a bed of red roses some flowers have more petals, are shorter or taller and are in different stages of maturity. The same is true among animals, not only in physique but in temperament as well. Another way of understanding unity in diversity is through analogy to the human body. The organs are extremely different from each other, each performing a unique function that the others cannot perform. Yet this diversity is the very basis of a coordinated and healthful life system for the human being. Imagine what life would be like if every rock was the same size, weight, color and shape; if all vegetables and fruits tasted alike; if every flower had the same scent; and every person thought, walked, and felt the same way. Uniformity would turn our world into a prison made of mirrors and inhabited by protoplasmic robots.

Ideally, diversity should be celebrated. Unfortunately, that's not the case in most schools. They aren't equipped to deal with it adequately, because schools, in the main, are operated like pre-high-tech era factories. Boys and girls are placed on what teachers call academic tracks, a euphemism for assembly lines. There are high quality, average quality, and poor quality tracks — all carefully monitored to make sure that each student ends up in his "rightful" place. The trouble is that the criteria used to judge which student belongs in which track don't take into account the many different ways humans learn best. Some students learn in spurts, some are late starters. Labeling a child interferes with his or her development, and is based on the erroneous assumption that all children learn the same way, at the same rate, and at the same stage, so that any perceived differences are taken to reflect different innate abilities. Through tracking, or streaming, students who don't relate well to the traditional way of learning are automatically classified as "slow learners" and placed on the poor quality track, or put in special education classes that are supposed to serve brain damaged children. In most cases, the classification process is, in reality, a branding — the student remains on the same track through high school, that's if he doesn't drop out along the way. Many do — because they become weary of being reminded every day that they are dumb; they want to strip themselves of the shackles of an educational caste system created by an institution that refuses to recognize its existence. They want to feel free to grow. But tragically they find themselves thrust into the world, lacking self-esteem and direction, driven by a need to belong and ill-equipped to create a meaningful place for themselves in the future. They are unofficially classified as human garbage — and deep down they know it. Breaking out of that social mold requires a powerful will, considerable courage — and a break. And some manage to do it.

Many of my students were high school dropouts who finally earned their diploma by passing the GED exam. They entered STCC haunted by their miserable school record, plagued by a deep-rooted feeling of inferiority and doubts about their ability to finish one semester in our program. But they made it, a good number of them graduating with high honors, and — more important — liberated from what plagued them in the past. This kind of result has been occurring since 1974 in a small department of an obscure community college while for decades students have been ground through educational mills not only unfulfilled intellectually and damaged emotionally, but worst of all, believing they are incapable of attaining what they once hoped to achieve. To be denied the right to dream by an institution that's established to educate human beings is a grave social contradiction, a crime that eventually takes its toll on society. Evidence of this condition isn't difficult to find.

Now, I'm not accusing teachers of being criminals, for criminals are aware of what they're doing when they push drugs, rob a bank or murder someone. Most teachers aren't aware that they are participating in a systematic dehumanizing process by trying as hard as they can to follow the antiquated educational philosophy and guidelines of a school system that provides them with a weekly check. When a lot of effort is expended to educate a group of students and they make little headway, many teachers eventually give up trying and assume, unofficially of course, a caretaker role whose primary aim is to maintain classroom tranquility.

If maintaining order is the primary criterion in running a school, then Springfield, Massachusetts' Commerce High School, would have to be classified a model academic institution. To Dr. Phyllis Gudger-Porter, who taught English there for a year, Commerce was more like a cemetery than a school. It was apparent the first day on the job that her colleagues had given up on their students. They created an illusion that their students were deeply involved in academic pursuit by making them do busy work that did little to develop their thinking potential and arouse a love for learning. A favorite classroom exercise was to have students copy verbatim several chapters from classical novels. At the beginning of the class the students would open their notebooks and start writing, stopping only when the bell rang at the end of the period. There was no homework. Grades were based on the orderliness of the notebooks and on whether all that was supposed to be copied was actually copied. Most of the students received A's and B's, and graduated high school reading and writing on at best an eighth grade level, unprepared for college or to do the kind of work that high-tech industries demand.

What also infuriated Dr. Gudger-Porter was the incessant gossip that took place in the teachers' lounge about some of their students, who were unjustly categorized, a classification that would follow them from class to class and from grade to grade. Because what Dr. Gudger-Porter experienced is taking place in thousands of other schools, most young Americans are undereducated. They are undereducated because they have been underestimated. And underestimation is the result of teachers being unable to draw out the potential of their students, and something even more basic than that — not believing that all of their students can succeed. When a teacher consistently manifests faith in his students, they begin to believe they can succeed. Conversely, when a teacher expects a student to fail, he usually fails. And that confidence-shattering message is usually transmitted non-verbally.

Why is this kind of dehumanizing silent interaction so prevalent in American schools? It has to do with a fundamental negative attitude that's deeply rooted in a basic religious belief, that over the years has evolved into a cultural convention. It is so deeply ingrained in the American and European psyche that even those who intellectually reject the Original Sin concept unwittingly practice it. For example, new employees must always prove their worth; the same is true with students. When a child deviates from what he's expected to do in school, an inner voice from the teacher's past whispers: "just as I expected." Now the teacher may not verbally humiliate the child, but she may have difficulty masking her feelings, something a child, especially one who already doesn't feel good about himself, will pick up. The child senses that he's being categorized. I know the feeling. Like all human beings, students need love and encouragement and to be viewed and accepted as fundamentally good. A child is like a seed, pregnant with great potential. With the proper cultivation and nourishment, it'll reach its fullest potential.

In most cases, a teacher's attitude determines how a student performs in class, how much she learns and, to a degree, whether she will be able to achieve her career goal. If a teacher is indifferent about his professional responsibilities, chances are his students will reflect a similar attitude, while a highly critical teacher, who treats students harshly, especially in primary school grades, can permanently retard a student's educational development and crush her self-confidence. I'll never forget what happened to a young lady friend of mine in the fifth grade. Though excelling in literature and history, and one of the best writers in our class, she had trouble with mathematics. Instead of trying to find out the source of the youngster's problem, and spending time tutoring her, the teacher often criticized the child in front of her classmates. One morning, after berating my friend for not knowing the answer to a math problem, the teacher took the child by the hand and locked her in the closet for the remainder of the period. From that day on, my friend refused to take mathematics in school, and because of that gave up the idea of pursuing a university degree.

Those teachers who possess a genuine desire to help all of their students grow intellectually and socially usually put considerable thought into creating the kind of classroom environment in which students experience joy in learning. Central to the healthy environment is the teacher's positive attitude. When the teacher is consistently encouraging, a student will feel comfortable to share her concerns — and not only learning concerns. A strong bond develops between teacher and pupil. When that happens a student's self-esteem is usually bolstered, which often results in improved academic performance on the part of the student.

But encouragement is not enough. A teacher's expectations of her students' classroom performance is crucial. Many a girl or boy who senses their teacher's low expectations of them ends up fulfilling those expectations. On the other hand, if a secondary school female student is made to feel that she can master physics, she will most likely do well in that subject, despite a nagging suspicion that "women have difficulty with the physical sciences." One of the reasons why teachers who have high expectations of their students are successful in the classroom is because they are willing to work harder. To get a student, who has a poor scholastic record, to accept his teacher's expectations of him usually requires a considerable amount of one-on-one contact, where a lot of energy is expended in breaking down barriers and overcoming doubts.

What happened at a predominantly Hispanic high school in Los Angeles several years ago is a case in point: a new teacher arrived at the school who refused to accept the prevailing notions that the veteran teachers, school counselors and the principal held about the school being essentially a storage center for wayward teenagers. The student body had the reputation of being "non-college material".

The teacher, himself a Hispanic, who gave up a secure position as a computer engineer to teach high school mathematics, proved those notions wrong. It took hard work, but he made his point. Though he had to teach the lowest ranked math students, in a year's time those students — female and male — were scoring high grades in Calculus. (A year earlier they had been struggling with basic mathematics.) They did so well in the national exams that initially the official test reviewers refused to accept the scores. They suspected the students of cheating, and ordered them to take another battery of tests. When the students did even better than the first time, educators across the nation took notice. Hollywood produced a film about what the teacher had been able to accomplish. The key to his success was that he never gave up on his students; he expected them to excel. In a sense, he breathed confidence into them, even when they tried to discourage him from doing it.

Many teachers who started their careers as idealists with a mission to become a positive force in the lives of their students are eventually drained of their enthusiasm and view teaching as a typical factory worker views his job, expending most of his creative energy in planning what he's going to do after work hours. Among the growing legions of apathetic teachers are men and women who still want to do something constructive in their classrooms but can't generate the energy needed to buck the creative-sapping and rigid dictums of an insensitive and visionless educational establishment committed to producing graduates who will contribute meaningfully to the industrial age. The trouble is that many educational leaders who recognize that we have evolved into another age are paralyzed as to how to restructure their schools to meet the needs and demands of the new age.

Obviously, to begin to organize a new curriculum and teaching approach, it's essential to understand the focus of the new age. While it is important to provide students with the latest learning tools like computers, it is even more important that the classroom curriculum reflects the latest scientific and philosophical understanding of reality. Today, for example, there is knowledge of our universe, our planet, of human life that wasn't available when school curricula and teaching approaches were formulated to serve the needs of the industrial age. We now know that our planet is invisible relative to all of creation; that contrary to the teachings of past great thinkers like Descartes, Newton and Bacon, creation isn't composed of parts but rather aspects of a dynamic whole or reality. For example, electricity and magnetism, once believed by physicists to be separate forces of nature, actually manifest an underlying oneness: a changing magnetic field creates an electric field and vice versa, so they are now regarded as aspects of a single force field, the electromagnetic field.

On a human level, every person on our planet belongs to the same species. But we're even closer than our membership of the same species may imply. All humans, without exception, are related to each other. We are at least 50th cousins. It is known now that change is a constant, that the only thing that doesn't change is change itself. I remember while fumbling through high school chemistry I was led to believe that a molecule was something solid and static, because the model used to illustrate it was a green wooden spherical object attached to a rod that was connected to other rods crowned with other so-called molecules. The same model was used to educate two older generations. Of course, now we know that molecules are continually changing even within inanimate objects.

I remember when I was attending school the nation-state was viewed in our social studies classes as the ultimate political entity. And most schools today foster the same belief, despite the overwhelming evidence of our planet becoming internationalized. Students who aren't exposed to the trend will be ill-equipped to function in the emerging global society. For it is becoming more and more evident that world problems require world solutions. Pollution is no respecter of national borders; nor is nuclear plant radiation leakage. Overcoming the drug problem will require a sustained international crusade; so will saving the endangered ozone layer that covers our planet. To stop the spread of AIDS, international intervention is necessary. For economies to survive, international expansion and open trade is required. And the idea of a world government is beginning to become more plausible as nations become more dependent on each other — even integrating their economies.

As nations grow more interdependent and gravitate toward planetary unity, there is a growing awareness that knowledge is interrelated, actually one, which scholars in the past, even great ones, divided and multiplied — and today's educational systems generally reflect. Schools still compartmentalize knowledge by teaching reading for an hour, then turning to mathematics; an hour later teaching history, followed by writing, then science. And in many schools these subjects are taught with the return-to-basics fervor that the American federal education ministry urges. The trouble is that this approach isn't in synch with the new age awareness of reality. And it isn't a case of teaching students something that is obsolete; it is far more critical than that. To perpetuate a fractured view of the world, a view that is fundamentally flawed is to perpetuate ignorance masked as knowledge. School curricula should reflect the oneness of knowledge.

For example, a curriculum could be based on exploring the essence and meaning of life. From this approach students would gain a meaningful understanding of the purpose of life, something most students don't have today, causing deep uncertainty and insecurity. They would also gain a better sense of their relevance to the rest of creation; and through that ongoing effort they would gain a better understanding of themselves, which would stimulate an appreciation for the need to grow spiritually and intellectually and acquire the ability to sustain the growth. Of course, basic cognitive skills won't be neglected. But they would be taught differently from the way they are presently being taught. Mathematics, science, language development, social science won't be viewed as separate subjects but as aspects of a dynamic reality. And every attempt will be made to relate learning to the real world.

For example, a whole unit could be devoted to studying trees because they are an important aspect of life. For most of us trees are common objects; yet they must have some purpose other than being a solace to the eyes. Before doing anything else, the teacher would make students aware of how trees contribute to human survival. The point would be made in such a way that students would gain an appreciation of how trees impact on

them personally. With that understanding, students would be
more likely to want to know more about trees and be more
attentive in class.

The seventh grader would gain a mathematical experience
by measuring the circumferences of the biggest and smallest
trees on a lawn and try to determine the exact difference in
size. Armed with the knowledge that all of the trees were
planted on the same day ten years earlier, the student would be
faced with a challenging science problem: Why aren't all the
trees the same size? Another science challenge would be —
why do leaves turn brilliant color in the fall in New England?
Or, why are trees used to combat urban smog? Comparing
human digestion and growth with the process of photosynthesis
would also be a challenge. Learning what role wood plays in
our economy, and having students list all of the products made
from trees that are essential to their lives would offer
meaningful social studies lessons. Having students prepare a
ten-minute speech on how they would have to reorganize their
lives if wood were no longer available would stimulate deep
analytical thinking. And having students write essays on how
trees affect their physical wellbeing would not only be an
English Composition lesson but it would also reinforce the
linkage between humans and trees, a reality that would have
been introduced at the outset of the unit. Tapping syrup from
maple trees, processing it, and selling the finished product
could be a rich learning experience encompassing science,
economics and marketing. Writing poems, composing songs
and painting pictures of trees could generate creative energy in
students. So would dividing the class into clusters of four or
five students and having them produce a magazine on trees; not
only would they have to decide on topics and write articles and
do the layout of the periodical, they would also create the ads.
To stretch their imagination, students could write fanciful
essays — such as "what would building a ladder to heaven lead
to?" By organizing a tree planting campaign in town, students
would not only become involved in a community service
undertaking, they would also have an opportunity to develop
organizational skills. The same results could be gained from

students building desks, stools, lamps and other wooden products — and auctioning them off, with the proceeds going to a local charity.

As you can tell, we are advocating extending the school to the community at large. Doing this will help trash the monastery mind-set that many teachers and administrators have concerning education. There are lots of things students can learn from institutions and individuals in the community. Many students sense this, but are unable to articulate their feelings. When given the opportunity to carry out an academic assignment outside of school, many students who usually do poorly in class, excel. They excel because education has been taken out of the realm of abstraction. What they're doing makes sense, because they know it's going to lead to producing something that will be of value to others, something that will have a concrete function. Learning multiplication tables makes no sense to most students unless 8 x 7 or 9 x 6 can be applied to real-life situations. Besides, the calculator has replaced the pencil.

Extending the school into the community can also generate positive social benefits. Some people in Bellows Falls, Vermont know that. When a few teachers in the high school organized a student-run daily newscast a few years ago featuring local and school news and sports, they were hoping that the students involved in the program would improve their writing, research, and organizational skills. While their goals were achieved, they had no idea that the students' efforts would produce bridges of understanding between the town's youth and adults. In unearthing news, the young men and women had to interact with adults — community leaders as well as merchants and average wage earners. Biases against teenagers crumbled. And the students developed greater respect for the views and positions their elders held. Adults were grateful for the news media service the students were providing (the high school newscast was the only source of daily local news for the people of Bellows Falls). And for the students, it felt good to be appreciated and to know that they were making others happy.

Why shouldn't students — everywhere — experience that kind of feeling? They could — by integrating community service as a component of the school's curriculum. Starting from kindergarten, children would learn to appreciate the value of serving one's community. In every grade, students would be exposed to a regular diet of stories about the community service exploits of others. Those involved in successful community service would be considered heroes and heroines. Ideally, students who excel in community service would be viewed by their peers and other townspeople as local football stars are viewed today. To ensure that this kind of attitude comes into being, the school system should prevail upon the news media to cover class community service achievements. In every grade students would have an opportunity to participate in a community service project, one that they create and organize, or one created by the teacher, or one developed through student and teacher consultation and collaboration.

In kindergarten, for example, children, with the help of their teacher, could produce a songfest for a nearby nursing home. Eighth graders could build sand boxes and see-saws for a local park. High school seniors could plant trees along Main Street. Most of the projects would be executed after regular school hours, the time sports teams reserve for practice and games. To lessen the teacher's load, each school would have a director of community service, with a small staff. Through a school-sponsored community service program, the town or city would become more united, crime would diminish and municipal budgets would decrease — but more important, a new generation of local citizens would emerge with an ingrained sense of altruism and an appreciation for sharing and service, which would be enthusiastically passed on to their offspring, thus ensuring healthy community development.

Effective education requires the genuine participation of parents. What I'm suggesting has to do with more than belonging to the local Parents and Teachers Association. It has to do with consistent and conscientious involvement with their children's educational experiences. At present most parents pay little or no attention to what their children are doing in school. They have abdicated their educational responsibilities to teachers, who are often in conflict over their students' parents' non-involvement in their children's school work. They're in conflict because the administration and the teachers union discourage parental interference in the students' learning process, supporting the "leave the teaching to the professionals" attitude. Yet many teachers — parents themselves — realize parental encouragement and homework assistance from time to time is necessary if students are going to have a meaningful experience in school.

Ideally, a teacher should meet with each student's parents or guardians at least twice during the academic year. Through these meetings a teacher could learn more about her students, thus making her more capable of motivating them. And if a particular student has behavioral problems, talking to his parents could provide the teacher with some insight as to the origin of the student's difficulties. She would then be in a better position to create a remedy. The meetings could also be used to educate the parents about the importance of their roles in the education of their children. A partnership could be forged with the parents, whereby the teacher takes on a surrogate parental role in the classroom. In other words, the teacher becomes the child's third parent. The kind of care and concern a child experiences at home will, to a degree, be experienced in school. Now, I know that in most cases it is impossible for a teacher to duplicate the kind of attention and affection that parents can give their child, but the fact that the teacher makes a wholehearted attempt to provide that type of caring creates some positive emotional continuity between home and school. Simply put, it is better for a student to have a teacher who is caring than non-caring.

Of course, not all parents are loving. When a teacher comes across a student whose parents show little interest in their child, that should be a signal for the teacher to reach out to the youngster and give him the emotional sustenance that he doesn't get at home. True, today's teachers aren't trained to take on that kind of nurturing responsibility. But you really don't need training to bolster a student emotionally. If a teacher is committed to educating the whole human being — the spirit as well as the intellect — he will instinctively try to fill the love-void in a student's life. The teacher's love will be demonstrated by becoming a steady source of encouragement, by becoming a sincere listener, by becoming a compassionate and reliable counselor who is willing to tackle a student's non-academic problems. Exposure to that kind of teacher will generate hope in a student who has been plagued by hopelessness.

CHAPTER
FOURTEEN

Bringing Morality Back
Into the Classroom

I know that for decades teachers have been discouraged from taking on a parental role in the classroom. The emphasis has been on becoming an efficient purveyor of knowledge, an emotionally detached disciplinarian, someone who avoids any involvement in shaping student morals. Teachers have been expected to keep all classroom discourse on a cerebral level.

I can understand why the establishment of this kind of mindset has been strictly enforced in public schools. There are those who want to keep religion, the major shaper of morals, out of the classroom. Others who were once the object of punitive parochial school punishment (knuckle beating, butt paddling administered by nuns) want to keep that sort of thing out of the schools their children attend. Professional purists complain that their job is to teach, not to coddle. And educational pragmatists point out that they are not trained to deal with students' emotional needs; and if they were trained to provide that kind of service they would have to be paid more; and besides, they point out, there isn't enough time in the school day to do it.

Nevertheless, there is a growing awareness of the need to reverse the accelerating moral breakdown in America and other western industrialized societies — especially in the schools.

When I was in the New York City area recently, I picked up a newspaper and was startled that a story about a student being killed by his classmate in school was buried on page thirteen. When I was going to school, a story like that would have been headlined on the front page. Then again, when I was in high school in the late 1940s the major social problems in school had to do with chewing gum in class, boys wearing their hair too long and wearing peg pants or being in the hall without a pass, and cheating on an exam. Today, teenage pregnancy, drug taking and pushing, violence, sexual promiscuity and alcoholism are the major problems. In fact, 25% of all American ten- to fourteen-year-olds are involved in at least three of those problems; and 50% are involved with at least one of them, according to the Carnegie Commission's study of ten- to fourteen-year-old American schoolchildren, revealed in 1989. John Chancellor, a famous television commentator, was so struck by the study's findings that he stated in a commentary that the problems highlighted in the Commission's report posed a greater danger to the security of America than any geo-political conflict confronting the nation. He urged that Americans heed the Commission's recommendation that moral values be taught in our schools.

What seems like a good idea or the logical n :t step isn't always easily implemented. Even those school systems who want to provide moral education to their students will be faced with the problem of assuring non-religious parents that their children won't be indoctrinated by a particular religious creed. And convincing teachers to take on the extra duty won't be easy. Many already feel overworked. A way of overcoming that objection is to provide extra compensation for extra work. A less costly and more effective way to solve the problem is to create a new curriculum where morals will be learned while involved in a mathematical experience, a science experiment or a history lesson. Setting up a special class that a student attends once or twice a week won't work well. Parochial schools have been doing it for a long time. Considering the moral condition of our society, their special instruction hasn't had much positive impact in the community. The reason why special moral education classes haven't worked is that most students, especially teenagers, resist indoctrination; and they don't feel that the special class relates to their education because it is set apart from the mainstream of the curriculum. Also, students don't like to be preached to and constantly told what they can't do. Authoritarianism repels today's youth.

Moral education should be a positive experience that explains, in a non-condemning manner, why morality is essential to the health of an individual and community. When education is not directed by a moral force, scientific knowledge and technological know-how can lead to the development of instruments of death and destruction. Most reasonable people know that.

What they can't agree on, however, is how morality should be taught. Consequently, little or nothing is being done and our communities are growing more and more amoral — and we know what kind of behavior that leads to. Because churches seem incapable of stemming the tide, public education, which interacts with children from five to eighteen, five days a week for most of the year is the logical place to create in human beings an appreciation for leading a strong moral life. Certainly, the undertaking would be made easier if parents became willing partners. But even if parents don't get involved, schools shouldn't shrink from their responsibility to develop in their students strong character. I'm afraid we no longer have the time to debate who should take on the responsibility — for the survival of societal civility is at stake.

For a moral education curriculum and approach to be accepted by a community, it must be based on what most people have in common and agree on. Since there's little disagreement as to what constitutes a good person, a curriculum could focus on those human virtues that make a person good, such as: compassion, patience, humility, trustworthiness, love, integrity, courtesy, thoughtfulness, justice, honesty, resourcefulness, dependability, punctuality, empathy.

For example, a very progressive school in Israel has adopted a policy that both focuses attention on virtues and encourages each child in the school. Each teacher carefully singles out a child in turn for praise for a particular quality they exhibited that week, such as their patience, diligence, kindness, etc. Over the year, everyone in the class has a chance to feel warmed by the spotlight of attention and approval, not just the top academic achievers, and these qualities are held up to the class as positive goals to strive toward.

Again, the goal of helping a child internalize a virtue would be part of a mathematical, science, history or language development exercise. For example, teaching patience to second graders could be done by the teacher reading a story and discussing it in class or having children grow flowers in pots. (While learning about the augmentative power of plant life, they'll learn to appreciate why it is important to wait while the natural growth rate takes its course. By digging up a planted seed they would witness what kind of damage can be done by being impatient.) Having second graders help with teaching kindergartners could also help them internalize the virtue of patience. So could a homework assignment that would involve working with one's parents in building something together that would take several days to complete. (This exercise would also foster stronger familial bonding.) One way of encouraging the practice of patience is for the teacher to praise every child's demonstration of the virtue. This is important, because children, especially those in the early grades, want to please their teacher, and they like positive recognition. Of course, it's understood that the teacher must exemplify the virtues she's teaching.

In order for moral education to be effective, the acquisition of human virtues should be stressed from kindergarten to 12th grade, with administrators and teachers always keeping in mind the importance of intertwining the teaching of virtues with the teaching of what is presently considered regular subjects. Teachers should view the internalization of human virtues as more important than the students' mastery of intellectual skills. It is more important because without the support of moral standards, material learning lacks a clear purpose; it may be misused, and may therefore be of limited value. It can become an obstacle to human progress, even a tool of destruction. Of course, the ideal would be for a student to make significant progress in attaining human virtues as well as achieving intellectual excellence. Such a person would use his education to help his community become a better place.

There are social scientists who have been trying to devise ways of developing virtues in children. Among them are Linda and Dan Popov of Canada, who are having some success. For several years they have been showing parents and classroom teachers how to instill virtues and values into children. Their philosophy is both simple and profound. It is based on the principle that there is no such thing as an inherently bad child. According to the Popovs, a child is born with potential, and parents and teachers have the responsibility of developing and channeling that potential in a positive direction.

For example, Linda Popov feels that, "if a child has a natural tendency for high energy and wants more of everything — more time to play, more ice cream, more books to read — this can develop into optimism, dedication and enthusiasm. However, if the child is mis-labeled, and criticized for these qualities (or left undirected), they can lead to greed, aggression and selfishness." She goes on to say, "Children develop self-esteem by being honored for their natural qualities and given the help to balance them out with virtues like patience and consideration."

Though originally designed for parents, teachers are beginning to use in their classrooms what the Popovs call The Virtues Project. Each week teachers try to instill a different virtue into their students. The book that the Popovs have produced, *The Virtues Guide*, demonstrates how 52 virtues can be applied in real life. With guidance provided by the book, teachers are inspired to improvise.

For example, one French teacher assigns words like love, compassion, respect, truthfulness, and caring as vocabulary words. Students must memorize them and understand their meaning. She also asks them to acknowledge the virtues exhibited by their classmates, and has them identify virtues manifested by characters in stories they must read. Another teacher has an exercise where each student selects the name of a classmate and makes a note of that person's virtues — and shares his or her findings with the class.

The Virtues Project is not only benefiting middle class parents and children. Various social agencies in Canada and the United States are using the Popovs' method in churches and community centers in poor urban and rural areas. The Kingcome Native Canadian band in British Columbia had the Virtues Project trainers come to them to train about twenty parents. Francis Dick, a tribal community development worker, has noticed a difference in the behavior of those children whose parents have had the training. "Two of the parents recently told me the course was a dream come true."

Chances are there will come a time when students who are acquiring human virtues will ask why it is important to acquire them. It's a critical question, because if a student isn't satisfied with the teacher's answer, he may give up trying to internalize them, resorting instead to pretending to internalize them.

A way of assuring student interest in the virtue acquisition process is to explain that potential virtues are latent in all humans. In a sense, they are like seeds. If they aren't nourished, they won't develop — and when that happens, a man or woman functions on an animal level. Armed with that knowledge, a person is motivated to develop his latent virtues. Ignoring that responsibility, one becomes spiritually handicapped, and is incomplete as a human being. Consequently, human happiness is dependent on the degree of progress being made in the acquisition of virtues. For the process to make any sense, an explanation of what a human being is is necessary (see pp. 168ff). When we gain an understanding of what a human being is, we also gain a better understanding of the purpose of life. With that knowledge, there is greater motivation to internalize human virtues.

In giving the explanation, the teacher must be careful not to use the opportunity to press her religious beliefs upon students. Yet she can't avoid describing the spiritual side of the human being. In other words, the teacher must be non-sectarian in her approach.

Harvard's Robert Cole, the world renowned child psychiatrist, recently revealed that for decades he shied away from the issue of spirituality in children. He now knows what a mistake that was.

I think I finally realized that there was a spiritual side of me that was craving for expression. I was educated into the secular, materialist world of the West and part of me had to struggle with that world in order to gain the personal freedom and the professional freedom to do this kind of work with children.

Maybe we don't listen to our children carefully enough. I was surprised and maybe I should take that as a lesson yet again that children have a lot to teach us. It's remarkable and I think all of us who are teachers and who are social scientists and who are interested in human beings ought to pay heed. I wish this culture would generate further efforts on the part of all of us to understand spirituality in children and maybe in adults.

I think that what we have to learn is that spirituality is a big part of ourselves.

I personally feel that ignorance of our spiritual nature is a major reason for the moral breakdown in our society. Basing public school curriculum on a scientific materialistic philosophy, which is now losing its grip on people, is not the only reason for the ignorance. A revulsion against religious sectarian bickering and warring as well as hypocrisy and corruption has also contributed to students' avoidance of studying the human being's spiritual nature. I can appreciate that kind of reaction, for there was a time in my life when I didn't want to hear the word "spirituality," because I equated it with religion, which I felt was a force trying to keep people steeped in ignorance and superstition and was the cause of human torture and bloodshed. I wanted no part of religion.

What I didn't know at the time was that beneath the barnacles of man-made dogma and corruption that afflict most religions is a core of truth that over the centuries has developed man's moral consciousness. Without it, I feel, humankind would be in worse shape than it is today. The Golden Rule, for example, is part of the basic teachings of all the great religions. So is the knowledge of what a human being is. By refusing to explore that knowledge I led, for the most part, an animalistic

kind of existence, though I admired virtues like love,
compassion and justice, which spring from the human being's
spiritual side, but I refused to attribute those virtues to that
source. All I knew was that they existed because I had seen
them exhibited from time to time — and that made me feel
good inside. At the time I wasn't aware that that reaction
sprang from my spiritual nature. Had someone told me the
truth I would have laughed in his face.

I finally recognized the source when I became a Bahá'í.
Discovering my spiritual nature was the greatest experience of
my life. I found myself freed from the prison of self, soaring into
realms I never knew existed, experiencing feelings of exaltation
I had never felt before. I was appalled when I realized what I
had missed prior to my discovery. In a sense, I had been dead.

I vowed to try to help others discover their spiritual nature
by explaining what a human being is. I had to do it, for I knew
that by discovering it, one finds the basis of happiness. And
everyone, I feel, should be happy — it is our birthright. By
happy, I don't mean a constant state of giddiness or being a
captive of escapism. Happiness is being internally secure,
having a healthy awareness of yourself, being actively involved
in perfecting human virtues, having the strength to repulse
amoral material temptations, deriving pleasure from helping
others, being prepared emotionally to take on whatever problem
arises, and acknowledging regularly your awareness of the source
of your state of wellbeing.

Remember my experience with the students at the British
job skills development center? And their reaction to their
learning what a human being is? It was like a blind person
suddenly gaining sight. Witnessing that reaction cheered my
heart. In my explanation to them, I didn't take a sectarian
approach. I dealt with their reality, their true make-up. I told
them things about themselves they weren't aware of. Oh, it had
nothing to do with identifying each student's personality. It had
to do with describing what they were composed of and how to
develop it to the fullest. I dashed certain myths which they had
held as truth, which had turned them into slaves of superstition
and hopelessness. Since I had experienced a similar condition I

could address some of their secret feelings — which generated within them trust of me; and they accepted what I had to share with them.

Actually, I have been doing the same thing with my students at STCC. And every year I get better at it. I guess success does beget success. Had I hurt people or made no headway in helping students I would have dropped my moral education campaign. My purpose has been to help them discover their true selves; and in the process, they learn to be more secure, self-reliant, focused and equipped with the kind of knowledge that can make them happy human beings with a genuine desire to serve others and their community. My purpose has nothing to do with converting them to my religion. What usually happens is that Christians become better Christians, Jews become better Jews, Muslims become better Muslims, and those who don't belong to an organized religion become better people. I have had that kind of result, because the students have acquired a reliable personal development map that they believe will direct them to the healthiest places along the journey of life.

Their belief, incidentally, is based on feelings, and an expansion of consciousness, that one experiences from spiritual growth. Most of the students start our program ignorant of their spiritual nature; consequently they are inward-directed, suspicious, fearful, preoccupied with survival and personal gain, prone to cheating, lying, backbiting and deception in order to obtain what they want — classical symptoms of an underdeveloped spiritual nature. Deep down, I feel, they don't like resorting to that kind of behavior. But when you feel that life is a rat race you try to keep pace with the pack, doing what everyone else is doing.

Over the years I have had scores of students share that sentiment with me. Unfortunately, most of the students never received the kind of moral direction at home that they receive in our program. And it's a struggle, for it's difficult for adults to change attitudes and behavior, much more difficult than for first graders. But through perseverance, fueled by a belief that they need the map in order to become a complete human being, they drop out of the rat race and choose to follow a more enlightened course. It's interesting that the most meaningful aspect of our academic program isn't part of the syllabus I must prepare for each course I teach. Yes, I have an unofficial human development curriculum. And many of my students are glad I do.

Take D. K., for example, a 34-year-old U.S. Navy veteran, about six-foot-three and 240 pounds. For the first few weeks of the first semester his sneering countenance and arrogant manner and sarcasm gave everyone around him, including me, the impression that he was unapproachable and unlikable. Two months later I noticed that he was scowling less. One day he appeared at my office door, asking to speak to me. It turned out to be a one-hour meeting, with D. K. doing most of the talking. With tears in his eyes, he said that, by my explaining what a human being is, he discovered an aspect of himself — his spiritual nature — that he never knew existed. He discovered that he wasn't an extension of his father, something his father tried to inculcate in him. (And there was much he didn't like about his father, behavior that he had already adopted and was deeply ingrained.) D. K. realized that he was unique, with a particular set of qualities, and that he had the responsibility of developing them. I saw him struggle in his effort to carry out what had become his most important responsibility. When he shared his victories with me, he expressed a wonderment that great poets must feel after completing a difficult poem. D. K. knows that that kind of experience is far more valuable than learning how to write for television.

I'm convinced that teachers must take on a parental role in class, because today's parents, by and large, contribute to the moral breakdown in our society. Certainly not in a conscious way. Burdened by the need to survive and "get ahead" in a highly competitive world, parents exhibit at home the effects that the world has on them. And their children are watching and listening — absorbing what the people they love most are doing and saying. Actions that we would normally consider natural and innocent take their toll. For example, the phone rings and a child picks up the receiver and cries out, "it's grandma — she wants to speak to daddy." The father whispers into his son's ear, "tell her that I'm not home." By carrying out his father's request, the child learns that lying is permissible, and is given the opportunity of being an accomplice to an act of lying. At the dinner table, a mother's remarks about how sloppy her friend is becomes a lesson on backbiting for the children in attendance. When parents brag about cheating on their income tax and getting away with it, children take that in, and the condoned activity becomes part of their own behavioral pattern. If parents were aware of their spiritual nature and worked diligently in developing it, they would feel obligated to help their children take a similar course, and the kind of anti-social behavior being exhibited in our schools and streets by children and youth would reduce appreciably.

My understanding of what a human being is is based on a point of view that a friend of mine, Brad Miller, and I share. I mention him, because in a published essay he wrote in 1989, Brad focuses on our point of view in a far more eloquent way than I can:

Life has surface — that's outside. Then there's soul — that's inside. I happen to think both are important, but I think soul is more important.

Increasingly, I think we Americans are caught up with surface things and less and less with the muck and might of the soul. I prefer the force that drives the flower to the flower itself. I prefer the water to the fountain. I prefer character to knowledge.

The things on either side of the equations are important. But to my way of thinking, unless families, schools, neighborhoods, cities and nations nurture the inside strengths, we become ugly and dumb inside.

The courage to ask difficult moral questions, the readiness to honor the full implications of spiritual principles and the vigorous exercise of self-expression are the imperatives of the inside. If we don't use these muscles, we go to sleep, perhaps never to awaken.

To see students awaken from this strange sleep, wanting to grow spiritually, and feeling secure because they have direction on how to grow, is a confirmation that what I'm doing is right, and creates in me a desire to urge other teachers to do the same thing. We owe it to our students to do it. For if we don't share with them the knowledge on how to "nurture their inside strengths" they'll grow up incapable of knowing their true selves, their capacity to do good and find happiness. And, really, knowledge is of little value if it isn't used to do good and find happiness!

What I share with my college classes concerning the nature of the human being can be adapted for elementary school children. The human being, I point out, has two natures — one is physical (lower) and the other is spiritual (higher). The physical contains the elements of the lower levels of life; our bones and teeth represent the mineral level; our hair, the vegetable level, and our sense perception, the animal, and our brain makes humans the highest form in creation. Only humans have a cerebral cortex, giving us the ability to be conscious of our consciousness. A dolphin, elephant or chimpanzee doesn't possess that power. Another distinguishing feature of man is his spiritual nature or soul. Our mind is an emanation or aspect of our soul, flowing into our brain, which functions as a receiver — and computer, if properly conditioned.

The soul, which comes into being at the point of conception, is a single entity that isn't subject to the law of composition and decomposition; it is formless. We don't know its essence, just as we don't know the essence of electricity. When electricity is funneled into a lamp we become aware of its existence and some of its attributes. Smash the lamp and the light is gone but not the electricity. Damage the lamp, and less light or a flickering light is produced. The same is true with the human brain — if damaged, the mind won't function as well as it would with a healthy brain. But the mind, which is an aspect of the soul, remains intact and unaffected.

As to the soul's association with our physical nature or body — no one really knows exactly. It isn't within our body or attached to it. The best way to describe the association is through metaphor: The body is like a mirror and the soul is like a light shining on the mirror. Should the mirror fall and break into a thousand pieces, the light isn't affected at all, it continues to shine.

Actually, the body is the animal side of us, which is driven by survival and reproductive impulses that create in us a predilection for self-centeredness and selfishness. Our spiritual nature or soul, on the other hand, is a repository of latent virtues, waiting to be discovered and developed. In other words, a human being isn't born a clean slate. Within our soul are divine attributes, gems like love, compassion, honesty and thoughtfulness. The fact that they aren't apparent at birth doesn't mean they don't exist. A person passing by a hill rich with precious stones has no idea of what he passed. With knowledge, however, of what is within the hill, he'll be motivated to discover the treasure — and polish it. Parents and teachers should be capable of helping children find and develop the divine attributes latent in their souls. When we're developing virtues, our animal impulses are kept in check for the most part, and we appreciate the value of doing good deeds and gain pleasure doing them. We function more like human beings are meant to behave, our greatest joy coming from serving others and contributing meaningfully to the creation and maintenance of a unified and loving community.

Everyone has a soul, but not everyone is aware of it. If we're not aware of it we rely on our animal instincts to make do. Life becomes a wilderness, and we're possessed by the dog-eat-dog attitude. We resort to violence to satisfy an impulse — or cheat, lie, and backbite to obtain what we want. This doesn't mean we should disregard our physical nature. Survival and reproduction are necessary impulses. Without them the human race would become extinct. But they need to be tempered. And that's one of the functions of the soul.

To be useful, light requires a lamp. Our body is the lamp of our soul. Unfortunately, many people function as if they are only a lamp and spend a lifetime decorating it in order to create artificial light. In human development, balance is required. Both the spiritual and physical natures need to be developed.

Without it, balance can't be attained, and man functions as a beast in the field. Actually, worse — because he has a rational mind that can devise genocidal mechanisms, which a lion is incapable of doing. Only humans can order, organize and maintain an Auschwitz, Dachau and Buchenwald.

For me, one of the greatest proofs of the existence of the soul was Helen Keller's life. Though at eighteen months she lost her sight, hearing, and speech, she learned to read, write and speak through her feelings. In time she became a world-renowned philosopher who inspired millions through her brilliant insights into what truly constitutes a human being. This insight was shared via one of her poems:

> They took away what should have been my eyes,
>   (But I remember Milton's Paradise)
> They took away what should have been my ears,
>   (Beethoven came and wiped away my tears)
> They took away what should have been my tongue
>   (But I had talked with God when I was young)
> He would not allow them to take away my soul —
> Possessing that, I still possessed the whole.

When the soul is being steadily developed, the body assists in the effort in a delightful way. For example, whenever someone does a good deed, and his motive is pure, a sense of well-being encompasses him. The good deed, scientist Ed Blalock points out, triggers a flow of endorphins from the brain that produces the sense of wellbeing or a natural "high." Interesting, how our Creator has built within us a means of rewarding goodness! Perhaps if students were aware of this aspect of reality, there would be no need for artificial "highs" found through drugs and alcohol.

Mother Theresa is aware of her soul. In fact, she would most likely say she is her soul — viewing it, not her body, as her reality. When the mirror falls and breaks, the light continues to shine. How does she go about developing her reality or soul? Just as Gandhi, Martin Luther King Jr. and Albert Einstein did; by drawing upon the divine wisdom that extraordinary spiritual figures reveal. Figures like Moses, Jesus and Muhammad function as channels between humankind and God, and relay guidelines as to how one should go about developing one's soul; the guidelines coming in the form of commandments, principles, laws and parables. Actually, cut through all of the dogma and ritual and you'll find that all of the great religions' basic teachings are the same. When children become aware of this truth, the principle of oneness is reinforced and community solidarity is strengthened.

The difference between Mother Theresa and most other people is that she continually tries to apply those guidelines to her life; and she views prayer as a practical way of maintaining the inner strength that's needed to continually develop her soul. By prayer I don't only mean discoursing with our Creator. Perhaps the most effective prayer is putting into practice the virtues we have acquired, and being of service to others. Certainly, what Mother Theresa is doing is a prayer, perhaps the highest form of prayer. What she achieves are answers to her prayers.

While most of us will never have the opportunity to serve on the scale of Mother Theresa, we have the capacity to do what she does in our neighborhoods, on our block, at work and in our homes. I don't mean that everyone should set up clinics for the sick and homeless. For most of us that's not practical. But we can develop an altruistic attitude that's expressed through service and joy-producing speech. For example, if our neighbor is a single parent, we should try to assist in nurturing the child; if a new employee arrives, we should go out of our way to make her feel accepted; if someone has nine faults and one good quality, we should forget the faults and focus on the good quality; if someone expresses hatred, we should express love; if someone begins to backbite, we should refuse to listen. All children should have that perspective. Ideally, it should be developed in their homes and fostered in school. Without it, our children are deprived of the most important aspect of education and are forced to survive the best way they can in a society that's reeling from a tolerated hedonism whose appeal is growing, and which most religious forces seem incapable of overcoming.

Imagine what could happen in our communities if children, who are steadfastly and enthusiastically acquiring human virtues, become involved in school-sponsored community service projects on a regular basis. Adults would be produced, possessing a devotion to caring for others, and serving radiantly in creating a loving and unified community. And their children would follow suit, launching a cycle of constructive human development that would assure a future of real peace.

"The problem is not the atom bomb," said Albert Einstein, "but the hearts of people."

CHAPTER
FIFTEEN

Challenging Prejudice
in Education

For decades our public and private school systems have perpetuated racism. Oh, not by design. It has been carried out by ignoring Black and other non-White contributions to our society, and emphasizing White political, economic and scientific accomplishments. In our textbooks, expansion of our nation's frontiers has been romanticized and glorified at the expense of the American Indians who were trampled and corralled by white men driving westward. And children exposed to this version of history were affected by it. I remember as a child when playing cowboys and Indians no one wanted to be an Indian, for he was always viewed as a savage and the enemy. The few references to Blacks were made in a negative light, usually shown as subservient, happy-go-lucky slaves. I remember a friend of mine, who is Black, telling me how terrible he felt when he saw the only picture of Blacks in his fifth grade history textbook. It showed slaves picking cotton with a white man on a horse checking them out.

Of course, today social studies textbooks have pictures of non-Whites in less demeaning poses. They'll even devote a page or two to the 1960s civil rights struggle, including a picture of Dr. Martin Luther King Jr. But the publisher's attempt to promote racial tolerance has little effect on its young readers. To the children of color it smacks of tokenism, for they can count. Devoting 25 out of 350 pages to Black, Indian, Hispanic and Asian involvement in American history is tantamount to casting crumbs to the hungry. As for the white youngsters, they can count, too. Many can't help but feel that Whites are the superior race when the historian who wrote the book writes very little about non-Whites. Also, learning about Dr. King's exploits in the 1960s can't compete with the race prejudice they are exposed to at home with parents who had been brought up with the kind of textbooks my black friend and I were exposed to.

Social Studies textbooks, for the most part, perpetuate racism, because they consciously shy away from exposing the grand lie that American racism — especially the Black/White situation — is based on. Publishers, who are in the business of selling books, test a prospective product's market potential. Textbook buyers often dictate how historical content should be treated. The preponderance of school systems prefer preserving the established story of America's origin and development, which is essentially propaganda. Wanting to saturate the entire market with their product, the publisher usually bows to the content wishes of the schools in the most conservative areas of the country. For example, what the school systems in Texas prefer is what the rest of the country gets in terms of elementary and high school history books. Consequently, eighth graders in the average student track in Amherst, Massachusetts, one of the most liberal communities in America, use a textbook that gives the impression that slavery was a rather benign institution; the civil rights struggle in the 1960s is skimmed over; the American Indians are depicted as savages, and little is stated about Hispanics and Asians. A parental protest to scrap the book proved futile.

The inequality in terms of money used for education by districts in America fosters racism. Children in well-to-do and middle class communities usually receive a better education than their counterparts in poor neighborhoods, for their districts have more money to spend on education. The best teachers gravitate toward the schools that pay the best and have the best facilities. Since the majority of black, American Indian and Hispanic students come from lower middle class and poor communities, they usually attend schools that are ill-equipped, and with less qualified teachers. This educational fact-of-life contributes to the minority student remaining stuck in the web of poverty, and with all the psychological pain and damage that generates. Poorly motivated and prepared, minority students attending inferior schools don't do as well in national standardized tests as highly motivated and well prepared white students attending superior schools. This unfortunate social phenomenon reinforces the carefully concealed belief most white people harbor — that non-Whites are inferior to Whites. Every time the test scores are revealed and analyzed the fire of racism is stoked.

Of course, I find the scores meaningless, for I know personally that if I had taken my test scores to heart I would have never dared to write this book. Unfortunately, the educational establishment still places considerable credence on the test scores, demonstrating little understanding of why minorities generally score lower. This pseudo-scientific attitude fosters the prevailing white belief that Blacks, Hispanics and American Indians are naturally less intelligent than Whites. Tragically, the scores and the educational establishment's real attitude toward minorities reinforces the lingering sense of inferiority that most minority students are afflicted with. It is something that's difficult to accept for them and their parents. Facades are created to mask the affliction. And I know why that's done, for I used to do it myself. The human being has a natural propensity for wanting to uphold his dignity. Two of the most common facades are creating a tough guy image or flaunting one's material possessions. The "Black is beautiful" movement in some segments of the African-American community is an attempt to address the problem, but it's making little headway, mainly because there seems to be a greater need among most Blacks to become "a real American" — which means partaking equally of the bountiful fruits of the American civilization.

Compared to their white counterparts, most black children are handicapped when they start school. It has nothing to do with genetics. And most teachers, especially Whites, are unaware of the problem.

Writer Hakim Madbubuti, in his book, *Black Men*, focuses on the disadvantages, which he himself experienced:

One year, on my birthday, my mother took me to a five-and-dime store to buy me a gift. She bought me a blue plastic airplane with blue wheels, a blue propeller and a blue string on the front of the plane so that one could pull it across the floor. I was happy. That following week she took me and my sister to Dearborn, Michigan, where she occasionally did day work. Day work, for the uninformed, means black women cleaning up white folks' homes. Dearborn, Michigan is where many of the movers and shakers who controlled the automobile industry lived. What I quickly noticed was that they lived differently. There were no five-and-dime stores in Dearborn at this time, there were craft shops. This is where the white mothers and fathers bought their children airplanes in boxes. In the boxes were wooden parts, directions for assembly, glue and small engines. Generally, the son would assemble the plane (which might take a day or two) and then take the plane outside and — guess what — it would fly.

This small slice of life is an example of the development — quite early — of two different concurrences. In my case and the other poor youths, we would buy the plane already assembled, take it home and hope it rolled on the floor as if it was a car or truck rather than a plane. In Dearborn, the family would invest in a learning toy, and the child would put it together. Through this process, the child would learn work ethics and science and math principles. And, as a result of all that, the plane would fly. I was learning to be a consumer who depended on others to build the plane for me. The child in Dearborn made an investment, worked on it and, through his labor and brain-power, produced a plane that flew. Translating this to the larger world, I was being taught to buy and to use my body from the neck down, while the white upper class boy was being taught, very early, to prepare himself to build things and run things, using the neck up. Two different worlds: my world — depending on working for others, and his world — controlling his own destiny.

The deepseated sense of inferiority that plagues most Blacks was highlighted in the late 1940s in a famous study conducted by Drs. Kenneth and Mamie Clark — both accomplished psychologists, and Blacks themselves.

They tested scores of black three- to seven-year-olds in Philadelphia, Boston and Worcester, Massachusetts and several cities in Arkansas. All were exposed to white and black dolls. The child was told: "Give me the doll you like to play with," or "the doll you like the best," (2) "Give me the doll that is the nice doll," (3) "Give me the doll that looks bad," (4) "Give me the doll that is a nice color." The great majority of black children preferred the white doll and rejected the black doll.

About forty years later — in 1988 — the same test was given to black children of the same age group. Despite a greater effort to acquaint Blacks with their heritage, despite ongoing "Black is Beautiful" campaigns, the test results were the same as for the one given in the late 1940s.

Refusing to consciously acknowledge the problem forestalls solving it. Living with a lie can create emotional havoc. When there's a strong impulse to escape, drugs, alcohol and sexual promiscuity have great appeal. The bad behavior in school, so often equated with black and Hispanic students, is usually an assault on an institution that heightens feelings of inferiority. No sane person likes the feeling, he wants to get rid of it; when he can't, he tries to hide it from himself and others. And when he's reminded of it by an outside force, he resists the attempt, sometimes violently.

Administrators and teachers should be aware of those feelings and how they come into being, as well as know how to eradicate them in the human beings they are charged with educating. Sadly, that kind of sensitivity and knowledge is not forthcoming in our school systems. There may be individual administrators and teachers who have that ability but are afraid to tackle the problem without the support of the school system hierarchy.

The problem, which is the direct result of racism, is real, and unless it is dealt with, those who are plagued by it will never experience true freedom and will continue to wear the brand of a social outcast, a stigma that engenders anger and rage. Even people who seem very secure and independent are struggling with the problem. A number of years ago a friend of mine who is black revealed to me in a heart-to-heart discussion that he was trying to overcome his deep-rooted feelings of inferiority. To make his point, he said, "When I'm about to enter a train, and I notice the engineer is black, I begin to worry about an accident. I never feel that way when a white man is in the driver's seat."

At a meeting of educators at Springfield Technical Community College in the Fall of 1989, The Chancellor of the Massachusetts Regents of Higher Education, Dr. Franklyn Jenifer — a black man — shared an incident with the audience that demonstrated that he was afflicted, too.

> I had to get to an important conference in Philadelphia, and bad weather had grounded all of the regular airlines in Boston.
>
> The only planes flying were the small propeller-driven craft. So I led my party to one of the feeder lines and waited for the pilot. When he arrived, I noticed my white colleagues felt uneasy, and so did I. In fact, I had an urge to flee. And all because the pilot was black. Had he been white, I would have felt more secure. I had no control over the feelings that possessed me. It didn't matter that I was black myself, held an important position in society and had earned a doctorate degree.

While people like Dr. Jenifer can talk openly about such feelings, most can't, especially young men and women. And I can understand why. Yet, they need to overcome their feelings of inferiority. As a teacher I feel obligated to help them do it, despite the fact that responsibility isn't part of my teaching duties. Frankly, I do it because, if I didn't, I would be terribly conscience-stricken. For I know personally what it is like to be a captive of those feelings.

Simply telling students — and they come in all colors — that they aren't inferior doesn't work. While they may on the surface nod in the affirmative, deep down their doubts dominate. In order to make headway, they need to prove to themselves that they aren't inferior beings. What I do is provide them with the opportunity to do that. They achieve what no other first semester American college students achieves: they write a textbook on communications. While I provide some guidance, it is essentially their accomplishment. Handing in their 50- to 100-page document is a proud moment in their lives; but more important, I can tell in their eyes that they are beginning to believe that perhaps they aren't inferior beings. To allay the suspicion that writing the book was a fluke, I provide them with the opportunity to write a 30-minute television drama and a proposal for a TV public service spot, which includes a thoroughly researched rationale, a set of goals and objectives, a production treatment, staff biographies and budget. By the end of the academic year their confidence level has risen; and they demonstrate a freedom of spirit that conveys to me, and, most important, to themselves, that they're not what they had been led to believe for so long.

This kind of rebirth experience can occur in other schools. Victims of racism yearn for it. But they don't get it. Present day school systems, by and large, don't appreciate the need for it; and even if some do they wouldn't know how to do it. Teachers' professional conditioning would be the biggest stumbling-block. Some of the educational methods learned in college would have to be shed, replacing them with the kind of spirit that drove Mehdi Firoozi.

The left-brain based curriculum, with its inane true and false and multiple choice tests, would have to be scrapped. To reach most students of color, especially in the "underclass" neighborhoods, a right-brain educational approach is required, mainly because the students are part of a right-brain culture. Most African-Americans, Hispanics, and American Indians exhibit a learning modality that is more intuitive than logical, relying heavily on visual information, and they must see the "big picture" before dealing with the parts. Trying to educate them through the established curricula and methods is like trying to force a square block through a round hole. And this has nothing to do with intelligence. Some school systems who genuinely want to improve the academic lot of minority students, find themselves trying to push the block through the hole with greater intensity.

What usually happens is that they give up pushing when very little headway is made, and end up secretly believing that minority students are inferior after all. What happens to the African-American, Hispanic and American Indian students in those school systems? They end up, for the most part, in the poor quality track, which is the academic landfill, where the system's human garbage is flung. These students have very little chance of going to college, because they have been led to believe they don't have the brain-power to go. And their teachers, for the most part, don't encourage them to try to ascend to a higher track, because they feel it would be a wasted effort. Many of the poor quality track teachers view their jobs as behavioral custodians — and long to teach the high quality track classes. Where does this leave the students? Locked in hopeless conflict. They know their classification, and they know that others know their classification. And they also know that there's little they can do within the system to change the situation — making many of them angry as hell. They're angry, because they resent being classified as a "loser," and down deep they know that the authorities' evaluation of them is wrong. Some rage against the unfairness. Unfortunately, such behavior usually leads to imprisonment.

Of course, there's always the exception to the rule. Dr. Franklyn Jenifer is a case in point. Though he ranked next to last in his high school graduating class, he eventually earned three college degrees, including a doctorate, became the Chancellor of the Massachusetts Board of Regents for Higher Education, and is presently President of Howard University, his alma mater. He was such a poor high school student that in order to get into Howard he had to agree to take remedial courses his first year.

John Thompson, who is also black, and is one of the most respected university basketball coaches in America, was so academically backward in elementary school he was placed in special classes for the mentally retarded. Through a sports scholarship, he attended university, graduating with a Masters Degree in Psychology.

Jenifer and Thompson were fortunate. But millions of young black men and women in the past and present haven't been as fortunate.

Racism also has a way of derailing those Blacks and Hispanics who are on a high quality track. About three years ago I was engaged in a campaign to end racial discrimination in a nearby high school. Our group had gathered most of the black and Hispanic students together in a local home. We wanted to know from them how race prejudice was manifested in the high school. At first they were hesitant to talk, because they were afraid that the teachers and the white students would view them as trouble-makers if they shared their honest feelings with our group. They wanted desperately to fit in, to be accepted by all of the student body and faculty. Finally, a young black man, who had transferred to the high school from a predominantly black school in Cleveland, spoke first. What he had to say broke down the reserve of the other students.

The young man — his voice trembling — said that in Cleveland he had been an A student in science and mathematics. He wanted to be an electrical engineer. In fact, he had won several awards for the electrical gadgets he had invented while in Ohio. Eager to make his mark in his new school, which had an excellent academic reputation, he decided to work harder than usual. But his eagerness was blunted by the racism he experienced in the classroom, the cafeteria and the hallways. He knew he was different, because he often found Whites staring at him, as if he were permanently sullied. He felt rejected. Oh, teachers and students said hello, but he wasn't encouraged to mingle with them. Feeling isolated, he grew inward directed, and became so concerned about saying and doing the right thing in class he became extremely taut and incapable of absorbing the teacher's lessons. His grades began to fall. Back in Cleveland he had been an outgoing, curious, bright young man. In Massachusetts he had become an introvert — and depressed. Wherever he went in school, he was reminded of his blackness. Not in words, but by the way people acted around him. All he wanted was to be accepted as a human being, as an equal. All he wanted was an opportunity to be himself, to feel at ease in the classroom, to feel free to focus on what was being taught and not on his hostile surroundings.

The young man began to cry when he revealed that he had been dropped from the college preparatory track in school. Of course, he knew what that meant — his dream of becoming an electrical engineer would never be realized. He had been psychologically murdered. And those who committed the crime are, to this day, unaware of what they had done to a fellow human being. Tragically, what happened to the young man is happening to thousands of other African-American, Hispanic and American Indian students at this moment.

There is a scientific explanation for what happened to the black student in Massachusetts and the thousands of others like him in the past and present. According to Dr. Kenneth Yamamoto, a noted health development researcher in Hawaii, the thinking capability of a student is adversely affected when he feels insecure, inadequate in the classroom, when he lacks self-esteem and is plagued by a sense of inferiority. Those negative feelings of self, he points out, shut down the brain's cerebral cortex, which is the seat of thought, and the *medulla oblongata*, which sparks human survival emotions, takes over, creating in the student a desire to either flee or fight. Those who end up fighting become "behavioral problems" in school; those who want to flee eventually drop out. I doubt if many teachers and principals are aware of this classroom dynamic.

The late novelist James Baldwin was aware of the psychological murder that takes place in schools across America. He saw it carried out as a child and as an adult — in Harlem. He cried out for help, often in anger. Though his rhetoric was widely acclaimed, his message wasn't taken to heart by those who have the power to make institutional changes. The classroom carnage continues.

Baldwin wrote about it: "A child believes everything; he has no choice. That is how he sorts out reality. When a child retreats and can no longer be reached, it is not that he has ceased to believe; it is that we, who are all he has, have failed him and now he has no choice but to die. It may take many forms, and years; but the child has chosen and runs to death."

This death that Baldwin speaks of is most apparent in the underclass of America; and we're not only talking about the inner cities. The underclass exists in towns and rural areas as well, made up of those Whites, Blacks, Hispanics and American Indians trapped in a poverty cycle. In many western societies racism and class prejudice are intertwined. Most people of color occupy the lower rungs of the socio-economic ladder. Cut off from the mainstream of America, the underclass of America is growing in size and anger, creating its own mores, laws and economies, one of which — drugs — has caught the attention of the nation's leadership, because its poisonous tentacles have infiltrated the mainstream of the nation.

Chances are that had drugs been confined only to the underclass communities, they would have drawn little or no attention, and been allowed to drift down the dark road of decay and hopelessness, and ultimate extinction. While federal, state and local governments are aware of these unfortunate people, they seem helpless in improving their lot. Neglected for so long, the residents of these impoverished areas seem, at first glance, incapable of functioning in what is deemed, by the influential in society, to be a respectable manner. From an outsider's vantage point, which is usually television, underclass people are burdened by so many social ills — drugs, AIDS, violence, welfare dependency, alcoholism, homelessness, grinding poverty, inferior education, fatherless homes and children born out of wedlock — that they seem beyond the point of saving. Consequently, little that is meaningful is being done to help these people. Though no person of influence or average middle class citizen would admit it, they view underclass residents as human garbage, and wonder to themselves why little is being done to get rid of the social blight.

But underclass men, women and children are not what the comfortable middle class perceives them to be. Beneath their seeming anti-social ways, they yearn for what all people want — security, happiness, health, dignity, education, employment and a loving family. If you find you can't attain all of that the normal way, you seek abnormal means, which can create serious consequences in the long run. But desperate people pay little attention to long term consequences. Immediate relief is what matters most. This became apparent to me when I visited an underclass neighborhood in Griffin, Georgia.

A community center director, who had managed to break out of an underclass condition, was trying desperately to hold together his center, which he and his volunteer staff hoped would one day pave the way to mainstream America for at least some of the neighborhood residents. The lack of funds and community support was discouraging — yet they were clinging to hope; actually, it was more like looking for a miracle.

Standing in the middle of the sparsely furnished center — an abandoned supermarket — he shared his vision with me. When he mentioned what he thought were the obstacles to realizing his dream, he called over one of the volunteers, a woman in her early 30s who had four children and no husband. She had embraced the director's vision and was spending almost every evening working with the youth. After a brief conversation with the woman, in which the director praised her, she went back to the young men and women who were seated in sofas and chairs that must have been picked out of a trash heap.

"I wanted you to meet that lovely woman, because her son," the director pointed to a well dressed teenager, "makes it possible for her to volunteer here. If it wasn't for him she would have to work a second job to support her family, and she wouldn't be able to volunteer here."

"How does he help out?"

"He's a dope pusher."

I was flabbergasted. He looked like such a nice kid.

The director sensed how I felt. "It's hard to believe, I know.

And you're probably wondering why his mother doesn't demand that he stop pushing drugs."

"That's right."

"He's doing it because he feels it's the only way he can keep his family financially secure. Before he started selling dope, his mother had to walk two miles to work regardless of what the weather was like. Now she has a car. His brothers and sisters can have decent winter coats — and food on the table."

"But he's doing something illegal and one of these days he's going to be caught," I said.

"First of all, in his mind he doesn't consider himself a criminal. He doesn't respect mainstream laws, because the people who make those laws don't respect him and his family. If they did, there would be no underclass.

"In fact, he believes that by selling drugs he is actually providing a service for the people in our neighborhood."

"A service?"

"When there's an absence of happiness, people will search for it. The kid really believes that the crack that he sells will provide the desperate buyer with some happiness. You see, he believes that five minutes of happiness is better than no happiness at all. And the people who buy the stuff from him feel the same way."

I can understand why most men, women and children in underclass neighborhoods have little faith in formal education. It has failed them, because it is insensitive to their condition and needs, and is too rigid to change its ways. Consequently, they consider formal education, as it is presently structured and practiced, an instrument of their oppression. This doesn't mean that they're opposed to learning. What they want to learn is how to free themselves from a life of unending misery that their parents and grandparents before them had to endure. They know what it's like outside of the underclass. They see it every day on television. And they want some of it; not only the material comfort, but more important, the freedom to fulfill their dreams. For them, especially the young adults and youth, there isn't much time before they're permanently drawn into the spirit-crushing poverty cycle that has entrapped previous generations.

As a consequence, drastic measures are necessary in order to save them.

I feel there is a way to help. How it is done will take special care, special sensitivity, and unflinching altruism. Mobilizing a massive missionary type of campaign will fail, because underclass people, like everyone else, don't want to be pitied — they have pride. Oh, they will most likely take the handout but won't take the message that comes along with it, even though in some instances they'll pretend they have. Also, this kind of help makes the recipient more dependent, when down deep he knows he should become more independent.

I believe an educational campaign has to be organized, one that takes into account the real conditions in the underclass neighborhood. Because of the distrust of the Establishment, white people are viewed with deep suspicion among impoverished Blacks. Though it is important to overcome their suspicion, the way to assure overcoming it is to avoid dealing with it at the outset. What has to be stressed in the beginning is self-esteem development, eliminating feelings of inferiority, moral growth, and gaining confidence. When meaningful progress is made along those lines, a student will be able to see why suspicion is harmful to community development, and will be motivated to rid himself of it. He or she would be in a better frame of mind to explore the principle of the oneness of humankind.

Along with character development, academic skills will be taught, but not in the traditional manner. The teachers must be able to employ when necessary "right-brain" approaches; relate learning to the real world; and the curriculum should reflect the new age understanding of reality, not the fragmented and flawed view that was organized in a past age and is still being practiced in most American school systems. Obviously, special teachers are required. First, they must be able to relate effectively with their students. In a black underclass neighborhood, most white teachers, regardless of their good intentions, would have difficulty succeeding in the classroom. Remember, in the beginning, the idea is not to try to overcome the students' suspicion.

The black teachers would be developed from a corps of black college student volunteers who after graduation would spend two years in black neighborhood schools. The professionals they would replace would have a choice: stay on and be retrained, relocate outside of the underclass neighborhood, or retire.

The government would pay for the volunteers' college tuition and living expenses. The special training would be structured like the military's ROTC program. The volunteers would take one teacher training course a semester for four years, and spend their summers in specially arranged paid practicums in underclass neighborhoods. The practicums would condition the students for their two years of teaching service. A specially devised promotional campaign would be organized to motivate black college students to join the corps. Only those who are properly motivated would be accepted.

The black university and college would be the likely place for volunteer recruitment. Black scholars and educators would draft the training curriculum and direct the program. They would also create the curriculum used in the underclass learning centers. What the volunteer service would do, among other things, is build bridges between the mainstream and underclass — bridges that would become a way to freedom. At this point there are no reliable bridges.

To succeed, the federal government must make a Marshall Plan type of commitment. It must be willing to fund the campaign until the social ills that afflict the underclass neighborhoods are conquered. It may take ten years or more to achieve. But it has to be done, because if a merely half-hearted effort is made, the government will demonstrate once again to minority people that it doesn't have the will to end racism in America. For desperate people, who are beginning to show signs of hope, rejection could set off a drastic response. And to do nothing, and allow the underclass to grow in size and anger, could lead to a time when the streets of America will flow with blood — in cities across the land, and not only in Black neighborhoods.

Ideally, fear shouldn't be the reason for organizing an all-out campaign. It should be done because we want to help end the pitiful plight of a sizeable segment of our society. The Black students need to strengthen their self-esteem, develop greater self-respect, and overcome feelings of inferiority. All of that is a prerequisite to intellectual growth. Having strong black role models as teachers is a way to achieve that end. I know civil rights purists, who worked hard to end racial segregation in America, would view what I suggest as a classic case of social regression. Frankly, I surprised myself that I would take such a position, for as a Bahá'í, I believe in the oneness of humankind, and am actively working to unite the human family where I live and work. I believe in racial integration in schools, and I'm sure that in integrated middle class neighborhoods there are black students who are doing well academically. But that's not the case in the black underclass sections of our cities. The public school systems have failed the youngsters there, especially the males. For example, in Milwaukee in 1990, 94% of the students expelled from the school system were black males. The same thing is happening in many other cities across the country.

The plain fact is that the established school systems aren't equipped to do what has to be done. Why can't they do the job? They lack the will to do it. Why is that the case? The school systems are products of a racist society. I know in theory what I advocate is wrong, but the grave nature of the situation doesn't allow for a debate on the philosophic merit of operating all-black schools in black underclass neighborhoods. Children are being destroyed. By continuing to funnel them into the existing educational institutions they are being sentenced to a life of despair and hopelessness in which drugs, violence and rage are the only outlets. To end this murderous cycle, drastic measures are required. My hope is that those who are saved from the fate of their fathers will produce children who will benefit from a school integration plan I propose later in this chapter.

Those living in African-American underclass neighborhoods are not the only victims of racism. In America, we are all infected with and affected by the social disease. While most Americans won't accept that assessment, they can't dispute the fact that racism is a serious problem in their country. Why haven't we made substantial progress in eliminating racism? We have failed to get to the core of the problem. Many of us thought that through the long-needed legislation passed in the 1960s we had solved the problem. We can, of course, cite the gains made by some people of color in the political, judicial, military and corporate arenas.

The problem persists because we have avoided addressing it for what it really is — a social disease, virulent and infectious, woven into the moral and spiritual fabric of society, passed from parents to children, from one generation to another, for over three centuries. The civil rights laws failed to thwart the growth of the cancer of racism, because it only dealt with two of the disease's symptoms — segregation and discrimination — but not the disease itself.

Because the disease has not really been dealt with, Whites have found ways of circumventing the good laws. There has been the white flight to the suburbs, leaving the city schools populated largely by minorities and those few Whites that are too poor to flee. The best teachers have also fled to the suburbs, leaving the city schools not only segregated for the most part, but with teachers who lack the training and skills of those who left. In small towns and rural areas, private academies have arisen to block racial integration in education.

Growing up in a community afflicted by even subtle racism fosters an adversarial attitude, an "us versus them" mentality that is acted out on the job, in school, on the playground, and even in church. In time the attitude becomes a deeply rooted obstacle to attaining real social unity.

The consequences go beyond disrupting social cohesion, however. The United States is undergoing a demographic transition in which an increasing fraction of the work force are minorities and immigrants. The jobs being created today require a lot of education and skill compared to the jobs of previous generations. Racism, which results in the denial of quality education for minorities, will increasingly exacerbate the crisis of human capital and further jeopardize the economic vitality of the United States.

The "us versus them" attitude fostered by racism also has international consequences. It is carried into political affairs by those who grow up in our society and ultimately becomes a barrier to world peace. Indeed, many international problems parallel the problems of *de facto* segregation by race in America. Addressing the problem is necessary in order for us to live successfully in a multiracial country and a multiracial world.

What is the cause of the disease of racism? The cause is the Whites' inherent and at times subconscious feeling of superiority toward Blacks and other non-Whites. Everyone is affected. For example, it creates a sense of inferiority among people of color which inhibits their development and self-empowerment. It is such a powerful disease that it has even spawned a prejudice within the black community against those with darker skin. Getting most Whites to acknowledge that they are infected by the disease is difficult, because most of them recognize intellectually that racism is bad, and they do not want to be associated with something that is universally recognized as evil. So many white men and women, people of goodwill, are repressing their true feelings about people of color under the hard-shell of denial, a major obstacle to overcoming racism. Cracking open the shell and finally acl iowledging the truth can be painful, but in time the pain subsides as progress is made in the healing process. What is important is the recognition of the personal problem, for without that there can be no solution.

Education can play a significant role in curing the disease of racism in America. Since racism is based on the myth of White superiority and non-White inferiority, schools can make a conscious effort to expose the deeply entrenched lie that has been embraced as the truth by the great majority of Americans for more than 300 years. To do this, schools must familiarize students with the reality of the oneness of the human family. Because of the magnitude of the problem, this theme should be woven into the school system's curriculum from kindergarten through the 12th grade, and reflected in every course a child takes for twelve years, even electives such as art, music, home economics and auto mechanics.

This approach will act as a shield against racism. Imagine kindergartners, black, white, Hispanic, Asian-American and American Indian, learning about the oneness of the human family, learning that their classmates are actually relatives. The seeds of truth will have been planted in five-year-old minds and nourished for the next twelve years. They will be fortified to repulse the poison of prejudice that they are exposed to in their homes and in the street.

Providing a step-by-step pattern for promoting the oneness of the human family in the classroom wouldn't be wise, for each class is different and every teacher should have the freedom to create an approach with which he feels comfortable. (For those who lack confidence, there is a document, *Healing Racism: Education's Role,** that provides some guidance on how to organize a procedure.) What is most important, however, is that the teachers have the will and commitment to carry out the responsibility to help students understand and internalize the reality of the oneness of the human family.

A committed administration can generate teacher commitment. Usually, when a superintendent of schools is enthusiastic about a pedagogical concept, he or she is able to persuade principals to adopt and vigorously promote the concept in their schools. In order to persuade the teachers to integrate the oneness theme into the curriculum, the principal must emphasize the need. In doing this, it is important to keep in mind that commitment is mainly an emotional response springing from conviction.

Granted, making a commitment will not be easy because it requires an honest appraisal of one's real feelings about race. Many may be reluctant to undertake such an appraisal for fear of what will be discovered. Most teachers and administrators are people of goodwill who recognize racism as something evil; they do not want to be associated with it in any way. This leads to denial, which is a major stumbling-block in the battle to eliminate racism in America.

If teachers understood that racism is a social disease, dealing with it on a personal basis would be less threatening. A person is

*Available from Oneworld Publications, US $5/£3 incl. p&p.

not evil because he has pneumonia; he seeks a remedy, applies it, and eventually heals himself. The overt bigot, who flaunts his racism, suffers from an ugly form of this disease. Most teachers, however, do not fall into this category, nor is this the form of racism that we are most concerned with here.

Most white American teachers have been affected by racism in a much more subtle way. Although they may have a genuine love for members of another race, they often harbor a subconscious sense of superiority toward them which manifests itself in a patronizing manner. While they may be unaware of such patterns in their own behavior in classrooms and hallways, it is usually obvious to the victims of racism. The patronizing behavior rankles Blacks, Hispanics, Asian-Americans and Native Americans. It is this subconscious feeling of superiority on the part of Whites, which is part of the dominant American culture that must be addressed.

When white teachers become acquainted with the gravity of America's racism problem, they will better appreciate the pain, anguish and frustration that the targets of racism feel almost every day of their lives. They will begin to understand that many minority students come to class already afflicted by the fears and uncertainties that plague their parents. The white teachers will feel compelled to devise creative ways of overcoming communications barriers that do not exist between themselves and most white students. By reading and discussing with their peers books such as *Black Like Me, The Hidden Wound,* and *To Be One* (all authored by college educated progressive Whites from the North and the South), these teachers might be moved to break through the shell of denial and come to grips with their own prejudice.

To help teachers and administrators who are earnestly grappling with their prejudices, the school system could organize and operate an "Institute for the Healing of Racism." Patterned to a degree after Alcoholics Anonymous, it could be opened to parents as well as all school personnel and students. Understanding how racism came into being in America would also help educators develop legitimate empathy for those who are the targets of the social disease. To be able to distinguish between prejudice and racism will also help. Prejudice is an emotional commitment to ignorance, whereas racism is institutionalized race prejudice linked with the establishment and maintenance of political, social and economic power. For example, racism is developed when a government encourages a prevailing prejudice toward a particular people in order to dominate and control them and gain something from them (such as cheap labor).

Armed with a more empathetic attitude toward minorities, teachers will be more willing to embrace the scientific proofs of the principle of the oneness of the human family. The school principal could make the data available through a series of workshops and lectures. To follow up, excerpts from books such as *The Global Brain, The Turning Point, The Seven Mysteries of Life, A Guide for the Perplexed*, and *Human Diversity* would be shared with the faculty. Such books should become a part of the school library. Ideally, every teacher should be given a copy of each book and urged to read it. Special items could be devoted for teachers to come together to discuss what they have read.

Weaving the oneness of the human family into an existing curriculum is a step beyond the multicultural education approach to combatting racism, because it fosters more than tolerance. It can instill in children and youth a sense of universal belonging that can develop into a lasting love for all people.

Racism isn't the only form of prejudice in our schools. There's a segment of our society — traditionally viewed as the "fairer sex" — that has for ages been held back by school systems from developing their potential to the fullest. I'm sure it wasn't done on purpose. Society's institutions, even religious ones, fostered the belief that the "fairer sex" really meant the inferior one. And for a long time most men and women accepted that as reality. Though now more and more people know that what was perceived as reality was a misconception, the damage done is still very evident in all aspects of life, including our institutions of learning. Sexism cuts across all classes. Rich and poor females suffer the same deprivations.

It is not only men who require a change of attitude and behavior, but many women as well. The brainwashing that took place over the centuries won't be undone overnight. However, knowing there is a problem is a good start to solving it. Unfortunately, there are still many community, private and parochial schools that have a fuzzy view of the problem and unwittingly continue to perpetuate sexist myths that prevent female students from discovering and developing their potential. Ironically, most of the teachers in those schools are women, but they can't be blamed for doing what has been done by their predecessors and supported by the community's school board and parents.

How is sexism perpetuated in our schools? Often the teachers themselves exhibit the effects of sexism. They are unwittingly carrying out a hidden curriculum, which helps to perpetuate sexist thinking in the classroom. For example, when a child doesn't bring his lunch to school, the teacher usually responds by saying "Did your mother forget to prepare your lunch today?" Or when a teacher makes an announcement about a forthcoming Parent-Teacher Association meeting, she'll usually tell the students to remind their mothers to attend. These assumptions are commonplace, because it is still assumed that the mother's place is at home. It doesn't matter that nearly 70% of today's mothers work away from their homes. Another assumption that stems from gender prejudice is that mathematics is a man's subject. If a child is having trouble with mathematics, teachers will often suggest that the student go to her father for help.

Because both women and men have been led to believe that working with machines is "man's work," female teachers have a tendency to avoid operating anything mechanical in the classroom. When a male audio-visual technician comes into the classroom to operate a machine, the students get the message. The established teaching approach is another example of male dominance in education. Often female teachers will disregard their natural other-supportive communications style, and resort to lecturing, the more self-assertive style, the one that men find comfortable. When that happens, the students are deprived of their teacher's best effort. They also learn that the man's way of doing things is the "best" way.

The curriculum also reinforces sexism in the classroom. Certainly not in an overt manner. In studying history, for example, the students are left with the impression that men are the most important decision-makers and chief opinion-shapers in society, because teachers usually emphasize the contributions made by the Thomas Jeffersons and Oliver Cromwells of the world, paying little or no attention to women's contributions to the development of societies, and the textbooks usually reflect that attitude. The same is true in literature. The emphasis is usually on what Shakespeare or Faulkner produced. Female writers often used male pseudonyms, writers like George Sand and George Eliot. Otherwise they would never have been published.

In science, very little effort is made to point out what women have been able to achieve, because it is understood that the discipline requires characteristics that are typically considered stronger in males than in females. This is based on the myth that "girls are naturally irrational, unreasoning and passive." Of course, Madame Curie is viewed as an aberration, and the contributions of female scientists like Ada Lovelace are usually overlooked.

Because of this myth, which has been accepted as reality by many teachers, school counselors and principals, female students are steered away from taking technology and science courses. Despite nationally funded campaigns to attract more women into the technologies, many of them avoid those fields because they have been unable to overcome doubts about their ability to succeed in a profession they secretly want to pursue. Consequently, most university engineering, physics, chemistry and computer science colleges continue to be composed of predominantly male student bodies.

More evidence of sexism in education is the way the western world's pedagogical establishment is structured. In most of the school system, women are relegated to teaching in institutions that conventional wisdom considers least important. For example, most primary school teachers are women, whereas most university faculty are men. In Britain, 97% of professors are male. Even in the British postgraduate schools — where future leaders are hatched — male students outnumber female students two to one.

Schools have the responsibility to help young women overcome their doubts and build up their self-esteem. Fortunately, there are some who recognize this, including several powerful institutions, such as Britain's largest teachers' union. It is waging a battle to end sexism in schools. They offer several strategies:

1. In nursery and elementary schools, girls should be encouraged to play with construction, mechanical and climbing equipment, while boys should be encouraged to use the toys the girls normally use in the domestic corner and look after pets and plants.

2. In secondary schools, girls should have equal access to scientific, computing and technical equipment and boys to cooking and sewing equipment.

3. Single-sex classes could be used in some subjects, such as physical sciences and technical subjects, to encourage girls to take part in non-traditional subjects. In that kind of environment, girls would stand a better chance of overcoming their fear of subjects in which they have been expected to do poorly.

4. Compensatory experiences could be offered to girls in craft, design and technology if they have not encountered mechanical, electrical or construction equipment before.

5. In boys' schools, pupils need to be encouraged to become more caring and sensitive.

6. Assertiveness training and self-defense could be offered as options in girls' schools.

7. Encouragement could be given in school assemblies to pupils studying in non-traditional areas, for example, girls on engineering projects or boys working with children in the community.

While commitment of teachers is necessary in overcoming sexism in schools, creativity and a sense of innovation is equally important. If history textbooks fail to reveal women's contributions to the development of our society, then a teacher should do some research. One teacher did, and changed the way history is taught in her grade. Instead of featuring battles and wars and boardroom manipulations — the male emphasis of history — stress was placed on how societies developed. The teacher went to original sources like diaries kept by pioneer women, as well as letters and household logs. Through this approach, both male and female students developed an appreciation of how women helped to keep the pioneering family together, which proved to be the bedrock of American society. The same teacher shared a personal story about her grandmother, who had graduated from dental school but wasn't allowed to practice in her state because she was a woman. However, because of a shortage of dentists during World War II, she was allowed to practice, successfully treating men, women and children in her community for four years. After the war, however, she was forced to return to the kitchen. What students learned from that story was that women could do what they were told they were incapable of doing. The students also gained a sense of what it must be like to be the target of injustice.

Oppression of women, which is an institutionalized prejudice, is as old as humankind. And the school is the logical place to combat it, for prejudice is a form of ignorance. Isn't one of the major purposes of a school to enlighten students; to free them of the bondage of ignorance and superstition? In carrying out that responsibility, educators must identify those pedagogical methods presently employed that reinforce sexist stereotypes — like the "survival of the fittest" attitude many educators practice by engaging in weeding out the geniuses from the dumb-bells and quickly labeling them. In general, females abhor aggressive teaching techniques like that and don't do well in that type of learning atmosphere.

Teachers, males in particular, should *own* the principle of the equality of the sexes. To do that, a more empathetic attitude is needed. That can be gained by making an effort to understand

and appreciate the pain and the lack of self-worth that a victim of sexism experiences. When that is achieved, a teacher will become committed to combatting sexism, using his classroom as his social battlefield.

I know an eighth grade teacher who has made such a commitment. Teaching at a progressive independent school, his students have taken an active part in combatting racism in their school and in their neighborhoods, but have been woefully ignorant of the sexism issue. While the boys refrained from cracking racist jokes, they often told jokes that belittled females, and would make remarks in class that hurt the girls. The teacher decided to put an end to that kind of behavior by confronting a student every time he made a sexist remark.

One day a boy cried out "that was a terrible mistake" after the teacher pointed out that the 19th amendment to the U. S. Constitution granted women the right to vote. The teacher diverted from his lesson plan and spent the rest of the period talking about the equality of the sexes, providing scientific proofs to support his argument. After several other encounters with classroom sexists, the wisecracks aimed at females ended. In fact, some students became as passionate about overcoming sexism as they were about overcoming racism.

But there is an aspect of sexism that the teacher hasn't been able to handle successfully. Some of his colleagues say that the problem is more glandular than gender prejudice, but he feels that that's a convenient rationalization. Most of his thirteen- and fourteen-year-old male students treat their female counterparts as "sex objects," especially those who are more physically mature. The teacher feels that cooperation from the students' parents is necessary to curb the boys' obsession with sex, which is demeaning to teenage girls. He recommends tighter monitoring of television watching at home, and greater control over which movies boys and girls are allowed to watch.

In order to overcome sexism or any prejudice in schools, all teachers need to manifest qualities that are usually associated with females. In other words, teachers must be more encouraging, more nurturing of their students; adopting a parental attitude would help. Being inclined to showering praise instead of heaping negative criticism would also help. Creating a classroom environment whereby all students would feel "at home" would make them, especially the more reticent girl or boy, more receptive to learning. Cooperation, not competition, should be stressed. And, of course, love is the most important quality a teacher should manifest, for that can melt away the suspicion stirring in students' hearts, a suspicion that prevents them from growing academically and socially. Having a loving teacher can mean the difference between a student succeeding or failing. There's no doubt in my mind that education has a vital role to play in eliminating sexism. In many ways, it could prove to be more effective than the home, because the home has traditionally resisted social change. The schools, on the other hand, are supposed to be centers of enlightenment. If schools do a good job, then students can have a positive effect on their family.

If education fails to meet the challenge, then humanity's condition will worsen. For humanity is like an eagle, one wing can be compared to man and the other to woman. If one wing remains underdeveloped then the eagle won't be able to fly as far and as high as it is supposed to.

CHAPTER
SIXTEEN

The Ideal Teacher

It's sad that in a country as technologically advanced as the United States, the teaching profession is undervalued. Generally, the best and brightest college students gravitate toward business, law, medicine and engineering — more lucrative and prestigious fields than teaching. The saying, "If you can't do anything, then teach," is ingrained in most Americans. This, despite today's nationwide call for better education. This contradiction is indicative of how deep- rooted the prevailing attitude toward education is. When banks fail, the federal government comes to their rescue, but when schools fail, conferences are held. When teachers strike, most taxpayers side with the school's management. In Japan, however, both education and the teacher are highly revered; the best and brightest college students compete sharply for available teaching positions. The government knows that the future of their country is being shaped, in large part, by its teachers. Maintaining a competent teaching corps is viewed as a national investment.

In order to improve the quality of education in America, a national attitudinal change is needed toward professional teaching. A way of doing this is for the U. S. Department of Education — with the help of the best advertising agencies — to create an ongoing media blitz that would elevate the status of the teacher in the eyes of the public. When aware of how valuable a teacher is in improving the quality of education, thus ensuring a healthy future for the country, the average citizen will be more inclined to vote for bigger school budgets.

Though higher salaries for teachers will help, it is not the solution, for not all teachers teach well. Double a poor teacher's salary and he won't want to leave the job. Teachers are the roots of the tree of education. Weak roots produce poor fruit. The idea is to strengthen the roots. Educational leaders, especially those who do the hiring, must realize that not everyone can be an effective teacher, just as not everyone can be an effective physician, engineer or lawyer.

In sports, coaches try to find natural athletes to play on their teams. By natural they mean players endowed with certain attributes, like considerable stamina, agility, speed, strength, sharp instincts, and a yearning to succeed. I believe there is such a thing as a natural teacher. This person may not be a store-house of knowledge, have a Ph.D., have written a book, or scored high on the GRE exam. A natural teacher is a loving, caring and giving person who likes people of all colors and back-grounds, who gains satisfaction from making others happy, who views everyone as fundamentally good, who possesses a positive personality and strong character, who communicates easily and effectively, who is a creative improvisational thinker, who is per-ceptive and empathetic, and has a genuine desire to help improve the social and economic quality of the community he or she serves.

Those who view teaching as just another job shouldn't teach. Students aren't machines. When you break a machine, you either repair it or get a new one. When you inadvertently break the spirit of a child, it usually remains broken for the rest of his life. Conversely, a perceptive and conscientious teacher can find the potential of a child, share it with him, and inspire him to develop it. That kind of knowledge is more important than knowing how to spell well. I would never have been a writer had it not been for Mrs. Fleming, my ninth grade teacher, who saw something in me that other teachers didn't see. What she said to me in less than two minutes changed my life.

An effective teacher has a teaching conscience. In other words, she understands her sensitive professional mission, and has set high standards to carry it out; when she fails to live up to a particular standard, she is conscience-stricken and puts forth greater effort. A teacher who doesn't like people, or is bored with her work, has difficulty maintaining a teaching conscience. Usually, students in her classes don't receive the education they deserve.

Unfortunately, there are too many working teachers who have little or no teaching conscience, a condition often brought on by apathy and an uninspired and visionless administration. Considering the potential damage they can inflict on children, a mass firing would be in order. But from a practical standpoint, that's not conceivable. Finding the proper replacements would take time; besides, laying off tenured faculty is nearly impossible, and there's the teacher's union, which is very protective of its membership.

But action could be taken to relieve the situation. The school administration and union could forge an alliance to help slumping teachers develop a teaching conscience — by setting up special in-service training sessions. Obtaining 100% success is doubtful, for changing adult attitudes and behavior isn't easy. But even a 10% success ratio is better than nothing — fewer children would be damaged. Ideally, all of those teachers who fail to change should be fired. Wouldn't a surgeon be stripped of her license if she continually killed or crippled patients? The trouble is that America's educational establishment is so materialistically centered that it doesn't feel it is crippling students. It feels that way because it thinks of damage only in physical terms. It knows when a student fractures his leg, but is unable to notice how and when a student's spirit is broken. Ignorance of the human being's spiritual nature causes that kind of blindness.

To improve teaching quality, education should follow the direction medicine is taking to improve the nation's health, by stressing preventive measures. To do this well in education requires an administration that is willing to scrap the established teacher hiring criteria for new ones.

In order to be hired a person must really want to be a teacher. Ideally they should be natural teachers or possess some of the qualities that constitute a natural teacher and show potential to develop the rest. Those who are doing the hiring should be leery of rejects from other fields. Of course, there's always the exception — like the person who became an engineer because he thought he could make more money, but always wanted to teach mathematics.

The teaching candidate must not only like people but should have a nurturing nature — the kind a good parent possesses.

He should be tough-minded. By that I mean he should be stern with a student whom he senses needs that kind of approach in order to be motivated. Also, tough-mindedness is needed when students press for an easier assignment and the teacher knows what was given is best for them. I know from personal experience that when toughness springs from a desire to help and not from impatience or anger, it usually achieves its purpose.

Knowing what a human being is is essential. If a teacher thinks a human being is only an animal, then the chances are that his students will reflect that view — and the corresponding behavior. With knowledge of what a human being is, a teacher will know he has a responsibility to help students satisfy their inherent yearnings to know, to love and be loved, and to commune with someone. A teacher who is aware of a human being's spiritual nature will feel compelled to develop it in his students. By doing that, the teacher not only fortifies a student's moral base, he's also educating the whole human being.

A prospective teacher should know how to discover, release and develop human potential. This ability is crucial in not only helping a student grow intellectually but, more important, it'll help him become acquainted with his true self, a knowledge that's needed to build confidence and self-esteem. Obviously, to do that well, sound knowledge of what a human being is, is necessary.

A cultivated intuition is needed to be an effective teacher, for there are times when a teacher must know how a student really feels when he's masking his true feelings. That same ability can be directed to an entire class in terms of sensing the real mood and needs of the students. Such knowledge could lead to a constructive change in the course's direction. With knowledge gained through intuition, a teacher is also able to create an approach that effectively addresses a problem that a student is hiding, but desperately needs help with. I know how effective that can be.

A teaching candidate must know that the best way to earn respect from students is to respect them — and not demand respect. They'll learn how to show respect by the way their teacher models it. By creating an atmosphere of mutual respect, students feel free to ask questions. The more questions students ask, the more they're going to learn. When students don't ask questions, they're either bored or fearful — and not in the proper frame of mind for learning.

A teacher must be willing to be unconventional in his or her approach. If it takes swinging from a chandelier to get a point across, then the teacher should do just that. The desire to be that way usually springs from a need to use the most effective method to achieve an educational objective. Teachers who tend to take teaching risks tend to place their students' needs ahead of their own. Those doing the hiring should always look for that quality in a candidate, for without it, it's impossible to have a strong teaching conscience. Also, students prefer teachers who take risks, because each class meeting becomes an adventure, and the desire to learn is heightened.

Administrators should be more flexible about hiring candidates who haven't mastered the established teaching methods. If they are creative, and possess the qualities and knowledge already mentioned, they'll create methods that will be tailored to the needs of the students. If they teach three different classes, they'll probably employ three different methods. Whereas those trained in the established methods tend to be more rigid, using the same method in every class they teach.

Certification shouldn't be a requirement. There are certain people with considerable experience in certain disciplines who are eager to teach, but can't because they're not certified. Because of this restriction, Albert Einstein would have been prevented from teaching high school physics.

A prospective teacher should have the ability to make schoolwork relevant to the real world. He should also desire, and know how, to teach in an interdisciplinary fashion. To do that effectively requires an ability to work well with other teachers. Remember the example I cited on how many different subjects can be taught by focusing on trees? The math, science, English, social studies, music and art teachers should meet to map out a strategy, with each one knowing how everyone in the group will teach their particular discipline. This is important, because students should notice the linkage between subjects. It will strengthen their understanding of the interconnectedness of knowledge and the oneness of reality, especially in the lower grades when a single teacher will often be required to teach all subjects in an interdisciplinary fashion.

A candidate for a teaching position should have a new age view of the world. Without that view, it is impossible to incorporate the oneness and unity in diversity themes into the curriculum; and a teacher will go on perpetuating the fractured and flawed Cartesian view — which, in some ways, is like promoting the flat Earth theory in the 1990s. Not only that — he'll have difficulty dealing with classroom diversity.

A prospective teacher should understand the significance of emphasizing cooperation and not competition in the classroom — and know how to execute it. This will lead to a unified and harmonious group of students, prepared to contribute meaningfully in the community, for by being involved in a cooperative process students learn to be cooperative. Without cooperation you can't have unity; and without unity you can't develop and maintain a healthy community.

Of course, it's understood that an applicant should have a strong knowledge base of the subject he would teach. While that's important, some critics of education believe all that's needed to teach is lots of knowledge — and nothing else. I disagree. Teaching is an art. Like a sculptor, who takes something with little shape and gives it attractive form, a teacher molds an underdeveloped human being into a wise person. Her molding is not the force-feeding of facts; it is helping students discover, release and develop their potential and spiritual attributes. Teachers experience feelings of exaltation (like successful poets) when they're able to inspire students, expand their consciousness, and lift them to new heights of confidence. Not every genius is capable of inspiring students or imparting effectively what he knows.

One of the major objectives of a university school of education is to produce artful teachers. Just because these schools are having difficulty today in achieving that objective doesn't mean they should be abolished, as some critics demand. What they need is a new dynamic vision, one that grows whenever new aspects of reality are unveiled, one that defines and describes new age education, which is much more relevant than what is prevalent today. It emphasizes the education of the whole human being and his connection with the rest of humanity, and provides guidance on how to live in a global society. In the 1970s there were attempts to do that, but they failed. They failed because the curricula used ignored the human spiritual nature. Sadly, the failure set off a backlash, with many educators calling for a "return to basics." My sense is that that mistake won't be repeated in the 1990s.

What's also needed is the courage to junk outmoded philosophies and practices that would blur the new vision. Accomplishing that won't be easy, because professors, regardless of their political beliefs, grow attached to ways that have brought them security and success.

The school of education I envisage will have a sense of the future as well as the present. Its view of the future will be based on its research and development programs that will be carefully monitoring, and becoming involved in, the scientific, social, economic, political and spiritual explorations and trends of the day. For example, professors will be apprised of the latest breakthroughs made by neurophysiologists on brain development and will funnel the information to teachers in the field so they can apply the new knowledge to their curriculum and teaching approach. Presently, a communication chasm exists between the bio-scientific community and public school systems — who operate on brain function and linguistic data that is antiquated. As a result, there is a terrible neglect of the development of children's brain power. By building working alliances with reputable outside research centers, by properly packaging the knowledge they gain from them, and by setting up a reliable data distribution mechanism with the general education community, the school of education I envisage will be geared to meet the educational demands of the 21st century.

In admitting students to such a school of education, an applicant's spiritual development will have greater weight than his intellectual achievements. A straight A student who doesn't like people and is self-centered would be considered a potential crippler of children and would be rejected. The ideal candidate would be someone who is highly developed spiritually as well as intellectually.

Those who earn a teacher's degree — regardless of what grade they plan to teach — will know what a human being is; they'll know how to help youngsters between birth and six grow spiritually and intellectually; they'll know how to discover, release and develop human potential; they'll know how to help a youngster develop her soul, and acquire human virtues; they'll know how to get students involved in community service projects; they'll know how to integrate the oneness of the human family principle into a curriculum; they'll know how to help students think deeply and more creatively; they'll know how to use their intuition in reaching and teaching students; they'll know how to help students overcome feelings of inferiority; they'll know how to motivate and inspire students and help them set and achieve personal and career goals and objectives.

Should a school of education student master all that has been mentioned above and yet lack love, he'll fall far short of becoming a successful teacher, for love is an irreplaceable bonding agent. If a teacher fails to bond with her students, there's usually distrust between the two. When unqualified love is expressed in the classroom, both teacher and students are caught up in a wavelength that transcends material differences and barriers. In that kind of atmosphere, students are more than attentive, they are involved in a process that is enriching them, and they like the feeling — and can't wait until the class meets again. Love is such an important quality in teaching that the schools of education I envisage will provide programs designed to help students become more loving.

Because they will understand when human learning begins, such schools of education will have programs that will develop special teachers equipped to teach parents how to help their preschoolers grow intellectually and spiritually. These same teachers will be qualified to help expectant parents organize and execute pre-natal education programs. Those responsible for training teachers of parents will not only take into account the latest findings of leading neuroscientists, but tribal fetal developmental traditions as well — like the ones practiced by the ancient Sioux. Local public school systems will employ these teachers.

A graduate of such a school of education will know that the primary purpose of education is to help promote an ever-advancing civilization, not to enhance one's professional career, provide job security, or be the means of amassing power and gaining prestige.

CHAPTER SEVENTEEN

Looking to the Future

Speaking on nationwide television in early 1990, the U. S. Secretary of Education called the latest public school students' reading and writing scores "Appalling! Dreadful!" Obviously troubled, he declared that "drastic changes were needed"; in fact, he called for "a revolution in education."

Despite the Secretary's impassioned call, few Americans have become educational revolutionaries, for three reasons: one, most Americans feel the term "revolution" can't be applied to their country, for only unstable and less developed nations have revolutions. Two, most educators interpreted the Secretary's radical statement as a plea for everyone involved in education to streamline the existing systems and redouble their efforts. To disregard what helped to make America great, they believe, is unthinkable, traitorous, practically blasphemous. Besides, some of them argue, what would replace what we already have? Unorthodox systems produced by elements of the lunatic fringe? Finally, most of those who agree with the Secretary are afraid to participate in a revolution, for it could upset their comfortable professional set-up and lifestyle. So they meekly cheer on the Secretary without lifting a finger to scrap the present failing system and draft more relevant ones.

Nevertheless, the lack of enthusiasm to raise the banner of revolution doesn't mean that teachers and administrators aren't aware of the challenge that confronts them. Some educational analysts reacted quickly to the Secretary's emotional reaction, offering an instantaneous diagnosis and cure; the solution to the problem is reducing a child's TV watching, greater parental supervision and more homework, they said. While this suggestion has some merit, it reflects a lack of understanding of the complexity and gravity of the problem.

The education community's flat response to the secretary's call doesn't negate the fact that he is right. When Dwight Allen made a similar call in the early 1970s, he was dubbed an alarmist, a weird academic experimentalist.

What will force the education community *en masse* to engage in an organic change movement? Further deterioration in classroom performance? But isn't that an awful price to pay, when you consider the amount of children and youth that will be sacrificed on the altars of warped professional pride and narrow-mindedness? True, but the record shows that it often takes disaster and desperation to induce fundamental changes in America's institutions.

As bleak as the prospects for radical change are, I'm optimistic that meaningful educational changes will eventually take place. But not by revolution. There seems to be a powerful force working in the world today that's breaking down barriers that according to reason and precedent shouldn't fall. The transformation of Eastern Europe is a case in point.

This force is being felt in every sector of life, using the most unlikely people to bring about profound changes. Who would have ever thought that Richard Nixon would draw China out of its ideological cocoon and into the family of nations; or that Ronald Reagan would negotiate and sign one of the biggest disarmament treaties in history with a government he once called an evil empire? Based on their ideological positions and past performance, they didn't seem destined to make such progressive moves. Or who would have thought that a cabinet member of a conservative American regime would call for a revolution? Not even liberal Franklin Delano Roosevelt, who tried to engineer sweeping economic and social changes during his presidential tenure, would have dared to make such a call.

This force is upsetting the educational community's equilibrium. Educators are trying to dig up quick-fix, painless solutions from the failing systems they're part of. Desperate, they grasp at the latest educational innovations. When they fail, teachers grow more frustrated. Pressure from disgruntled parents and exasperated governmental institutions intensifies. Cynicism abounds in faculty lounges.

While most teachers fear drastic changes, because they have grown accustomed to long established professional procedures, they are less resistant to talk about the need for educational change and radical pedagogical concepts. Though they are awfully defensive, and what they say is often negative, the talking is a means of fortifying themselves for what they know deep down is inevitable — the scrapping of the familiar for the fundamentally new.

The radical change isn't going to result from a single act — some oracle pushes a button and whooooosh, total educational transformation. The change is already taking place in bits and pieces. This book is a tiny part of the process, as are other contemporary books on education that address the need for change and make recommendations as to what form the changes should take. They stimulate thought and discussion among educators and other interested parties. The media's continual coverage of the issue stirs the collective debate. The search for the solution inspires a few courageous souls to create and experiment with new teaching methods in their classrooms, and others establish schools. While many ventures fail, some succeed, gaining the kind of notoriety that encourages other schools to adopt their successful ways. A spark can set off a forest fire.

Even those who vehemently oppose new educational philosophies are unwittingly playing a role in bringing about the change that's needed. Their arguments force the advocates of change to sharpen their views which, in turn, not only strengthens their resolve to persevere, but also helps to perfect the educational model they're creating.

I am confident that with this powerful transformational force quickening its pace, school systems will evolve with a deeper and broader view of reality, which will be reflected in what and how their teachers teach. I am confident because there is a loving God, whose respect for us is so great that he allows us to test the special powers he has given us. Because our abuse of these powers threatens our survival, He has intervened by providing us with guidance on how to attain His good pleasure, which is to try to love Him as He loves us, to use Him as our primary source of knowledge and to work wholeheartedly for the unification of the human family and the establishment of universal peace.

Education, I believe, is a divinely ordained means of carrying out God's guidance. In the future, schools will be plugged into it; love will be the dominating emotion; service, the primary motivation, and producing good human beings will be the most important goal. In these schools, someone like Joe, the numbers runner who schemed his way out of the Army, would become acquainted with his spiritual and intellectual potential and use what he discovered to help his community become a better place to live and work; the young black man, who was so traumatized by racism in high school, and as a consequence never realized his career dream — he would become the electrical engineer he yearned to be. Standardized tests wouldn't be used to determine a student's intelligence and ability to succeed in school and the work world. I cringe every time I think of my junior high school guidance counselor handing my father my IQ and aptitude test scores. Academic tracking would be a bad memory, a reminder of how brutalizing unenlightened school systems can be.

Parents will play an important role in their child's education — from start to finish. Because they'll be carefully surveying their child's actions, making note of his potentialities and establishing a solid learning foundation in him, they'll be able to pass onto the kindergarten teacher an accurate profile to build on; thus assuring a healthy scholastic beginning for the child. But the parents' responsibilities won't end there. They'll stay close to their child's teachers so they can exchange information regularly and assess together the child's progress through the 12th grade. To make sure that the teacher-parent partnership works, the teacher will regularly assign homework assignments that would require parental involvement. The parents' desire and ability to do all of this will be derived from special training that the local school system will provide for all prospective and practicing parents.

Teachers will be like Mrs. Fleming and Mehdi Firoozi — men and women dedicated to finding and helping to refine "the gems of inestimable value" within their students. They'll experience the joy and professional gratification I have experienced at STCC. I know many veteran educators would find it hard to believe that a teacher could feel the way I do about my work. But if I — someone without formal teacher training, no graduate degree and a poor academic record — can experience it, then those teachers who will undergo new age school of education training will certainly experience it.

Students will find school fun, an adventure, an eye-opening, mind-expanding exploration of themselves and the world around them — they'll have a sense of destiny.

What I envision most schools in the future doing is being done in a few places in North America. What these handful of educational bright spots have in common is a holistic concern for spiritual, intellectual, social and physical development. The Montessori schools, the Maxwell International Bahá'í school and the Wilhelm Schole* stand out in my mind as the kind of schools today's children should be attending. Sadly, most parents aren't aware of them. If they were aware of what they're able to achieve, I'm sure they would demand that the public school systems adopt what these independent schools are doing. In Cleveland, Houston and Milwaukee, one or two public schools have adopted the Montessori methods. An encouraging sign! Why spend lots of money generating lots of energy and waste lots of time creating new curricula and approaches when many already tried and successful ones are available?

As soon as my wife and I stepped into the lobby of the Wilhelm Schole in Houston, Texas, we were embraced by beauty, wisdom, and love. Prints of pictures of past artistic

Schole is the Greek word for school.

masters lined the hallways and classroom walls; tacked under them were printed aphorisms of famous philosophical, scientific and spiritual sages. Gazing at them set off an aesthetic rush in us and stimulated deep thought. We were captivated.

Every child that greeted us — and they ranged from four to eight — looked us straight in the eye, extended their hand and welcomed us to their school. They really meant what they said. "What poise and confidence," I said to myself. I have been to many schools and have never seen children display such manners and genuine interest in others.

I was to speak to about 20 six-, seven- and eight-year-olds. It turned out to be an exchange of philosophical, scientific and artistic ideas. I forgot that I was in an elementary school classroom. We were learning from each other. They spoke confidently about the Theory of Relativity. They quoted Einstein, Spinoza, and Confucius, and expounded on the discoveries of Pythagoras. They recited poems on time and space. When a student created a powerful aphorism on the spot, his fellow students applauded. Questions flowed freely: "What is your favorite culture — and why?" "How did you learn to write?" When they learned that I had written a book on racism, I was asked to distinguish between prejudice and racism. We spent about fifteen minutes on the topic. Everything that was said turned into a learning experience. A question on my favorite food became a little lesson on the Russian-Jewish culture. I love blintzes.

Time flew by. I didn't want to leave, for we were engaged in a learning adventure — which was free of posturing, free of rancor and acrimony, free of ego. We built upon each other's ideas. The room was charged with brilliant innocence — the youngsters demonstrating that they understood that the greatest moments of creativity occur when we are free of self — when we flow with an idea, when we concentrate wholly on tasks that lift us into a state of complete joy.

It wasn't a case of me talking with a carefully selected group of "gifted" children who arrogantly flaunt their knowledge. They didn't have to pass a notorious entrance exam to be admitted. The school is opposed to testing as a means of measuring capacity. Unlike most children their age, their latent brilliance is allowed to shine. The school's environment and teachers are responsible for that. So is the curriculum, created by its founder and director, Marilyn Wilhelm, who never trained as a teacher:

> The entire fabric of our curriculum may be called Holistic Education because we have no disconnected, departmentalized pieces; the arts, sciences and the humanities constantly interweave, bringing a unity to all our studies. Our students, discovering similarities in what is seemingly dissimilar, are making those leaps of intuition that bring understanding and cement the larger way of perceiving. Granted . . . intuition cannot be put into any student, but we educators can awaken intuition . . . feed and nourish it . . . and thereby develop an informed intuition. How? By presenting the disciplines not as a conglomerate of separate parts but as integral parts of an inseparable whole.
>
> Everyone — parents, students, teachers — knows the goals we plan to achieve. The competency-based system does not compare one child with another, but rather records the individual progress of each child as measured by the State standards and ours. If there is competition, it is the child competing with himself; can he do better than he did yesterday? Our schole is built on cooperation rather than competition.
>
> Our students know that a teacher can teach you nothing — you must teach yourself. Teachers can share everything they know . . . but unless you teach yourself, you will learn nothing. Our students are also aware that discipline means self-discipline. No one can discipline you but you. Further, it is the capacity for self-discipline that is the essential factor which elevates a man or woman above mediocrity . . .
>
> We believe the true test of the schole is the character that emerges. Therefore, we have defined teacher in a more profound sense: to teach does not mean simply

instruct; rather it means to guide, to inspire, to give courage and strength, to open the doors to the wonders of life, and to help us find meaning in our life and our work. Perspective is everything . . . and when teachers become guides who provide perspective, the school is elevated to its highest function.

Our approach is to educate children through the arts and to tie the arts into the sciences, mathematics, philosophy and the story of civilization, beginning in Africa, Asia, as our oldest cultures, moving from there into the Greek and Roman era which made for our modern world.

Furthermore, we place a great emphasis on language. We believe almost any child can thoroughly understand anything — but without language there is limited understanding, which automatically limits the ability to think clearly and creatively.

Every class at our schole might be described as a language class because we are always looking up words (every child has his own personal dictionary), writing poetry, or doing independent research and writing reports which the student then gives to another class. We believe in reading, writing, and speaking in equal measure. Thus the child is guided into a skillful use of language.

Moreover, we believe that at a very early age the child should learn that everything in life as well as everything one learns in school can be expressed in the language of beauty. (M. E. Wilhelm, excerpted from a booklet, *The Wilhelm Schole*, 1988.)

Tearing myself away from the Wilhelm Schole was difficult. I can understand why its students like school. As a child, I never felt that way; nor did millions of men and women who attended school when I did. Nothing much has changed because most children today feel the same way.

How fortunate the Wilhelm Schole students are, I thought, as we drove away. But as we began to wind through the streets of

Houston, I began to think about the countless children all over the country and all over the world who aren't as fortunate.

Yet it isn't impossible for children everywhere to experience what the Wilhelm Schole children are experiencing. All it would take is a shift of vision on the part of the educational establishment. With an appreciation of the approaches and methods employed by schools like the Wilhelm Schole, public school administrators and teachers would be willing to abandon what they are doing now in the classroom for pedagogical ways that would provide youngsters with an opportunity to grow up enlightened, secure and prepared to meet successfully the inevitable tough challenges that await them.

BIBLIOGRAPHY

Bahá'u'lláh. *Gleanings from the Writings of Bahá'u'lláh*. Bahá'í Publishing Trust (U.S.), 1939, 1956.

Berry, Wendell. *The Hidden Wound*. North Point Press, 1970.

Capra, Fritjof. *The Turning Point*. Bantam Books, 1987.

Cole, Robert. *The Spiritual Life of Children*. Houghton Mifflin, 1990

Dorris, Michael. *The Broken Cord*. Harper & Row, 1989.

Freidman, S., ed. *The Brain, Cognition and Education*. Academic Press, 1986.

Gardner, Howard. *Frames of Mind*. Basic Books, 1983.

Griffin, John H. *Black Like Me*. Houghton Mifflin, 1977.

Lewontin, Richard C. *Human Diversity*. W. M. Freeman & Company, 1984.

Madbubuti, Hakim. *Black Men: Obsolete, Single, Dangerous?* Third World Press, 1988

Miller, Alice. *For Your Own Good*. Farrar Strauss & Giroux, 1983.

Murchie, Guy. *The Seven Mysteries of Life: An Exploration in Science and Philosophy*. Houghton Mifflin, 1979.

Popov, Linda & Daniel. *The Virtues Guide*. Wellspring International Educational Foundation, 1991.

Russell, Peter. *The Global Brain*. J. T. Tarcher, 1983.

Rutstein, Nathan. *To Be One: A Battle Against Racism*. George Ronald, Oxford, 1989.

Schumacher, E. F. *A Guide for the Perplexed*. Harper & Row, 1978.

Scott Peck, M. *The Road Less Travelled*. Simon & Schuster, 1978.

Standing, E. M. *Maria Montessori: Her Life & Work*. Mentor Books, 1962.

Wilhelm, Marilyn E. *The Wilhelm Schole: An American School for All Nations*. Self-Published, 1988.